The Oak Tree

with

Golden Leaves

A Memoir

Rebecca Clarke

The Oak Tree with Golden Leaves

Rebecca Clarke

ISBN-13: 978-988-8769-83-4

© 2023 Rebecca Clarke

BIOGRAPHY & AUTOBIOGRAPHY

EB176

Published by Earnshaw Books Ltd. (Hong Kong)

DEDICATION

This book is dedicated to my beloved sons:
Charles and Henry

The COVID-19 pandemic brought seismic life changes to millions of people all over the world, me included. Without any warning, suddenly I had to stop my hectic daily schedule, reflect, and ponder over what I "have to" or "should" do next.

The obvious path was to continue my musical journey, to develop further my passion for piano playing, learning pieces that I have always dreamed about playing and studying in greater depth: the many great works of Chopin, Schubert, Mozart, and many others.

My thoughts were, however, never far from the summer Cambridge Programmes, which have been very much an integral part of my life and which, sadly, had to be put on the shelf temporarily until the pandemic was over. One morning, whilst sitting quietly to contemplate what else I could be doing, I recalled the pleasure of meeting one of the many charming parents from China. She told me how much her daughter had benefitted from joining the Science Programme, and that I had been an inspiration to her and to her friends who had had the good fortune to attend. She said I should write a memoir, as she believed many people from China would be interested in knowing about my success story. I felt this was a compliment which I am sure I do not deserve.

This idea, however, started to germinate in my mind and, as the end of the pandemic was nowhere in sight, I thought it was worth some investigation. I thought about my roots back in Hong Kong where I was born and brought up, my career paths which spread from Hong Kong to the UK, my marriage to an English husband, how I brought up the boys in Cambridge, and where life has taken me so far. I began to see good reasons why I should attempt to write a memoir.

Both boys have now grown up, have established career paths, married and settled. One lives in America, and one in Europe. They are only half-Chinese and, in time, I fear their Chinese heritage will slowly-but-surely become just a distant memory, especially when I am gone. I hope this memoir will be a record for them, and for their future generations. I hope they will be proud of their Chinese heritage: they have the best of both worlds, being half-English and half-Chinese.

I should also like to pay tribute to my Editor: Christopher Green. From day one, Chris gave me strong encouragement to write this memoir. Despite his many roles at school, with the A-Level Exam Board, as publisher of academic literary textbooks, and Trustee of the British Shakespeare Association, Chris still managed to find time to help teach on the English Programme, to be a Deputy Director of Cambridge Programmes, and to be the Editor of my memoir.

Tribute to Peter on his Eightieth Birthday

I just like to say a few words to mark this joyful occasion.

Today we are gathered here to celebrate an important milestone for Peter, Dad, the best husband and father of our two wonderful boys.

When I first met Peter in Hong Kong some 39 years ago, January 3, 1983, at 1:05 p.m. (as I was five minutes late) over a business lunch, he struck me by his impeccable British manner. After a few dates, I felt he was and still is the most gentle and kindest person I had ever known. Whenever we walked past beggars in the streets, he would always give them a dollar, from his pocket. Like a magician, the coin was always in his pocket ready to give.

Another very unique quality he has is that he never has an unkind word to say about anyone. He could always find something good in a person and he genuinely cares for everyone and anyone around him. His generous spirit was awe inspiring!

My initial attraction to Peter was one of sheer curiosity. I disliked the Colonial British who ruled Hong Kong intensely at the time. I thought he could be a wolf in sheep's clothing and I was on my guard. Sooner or later, I said to myself, I would find out. This was a bad strategy, I began to fall in love. Although my parents, my grandmother and my nanny did not speak a word of English, they approved my relationship without any questions. Peter was, and still is, that same kind gentleman I met, the man you wanted to spend the rest of your life with.

I was offered an opportunity to work in San Francisco. It was my dream since I visited that beautiful city a few years ago and thought it would be wonderful to work and live there. But to have chosen a life with Peter, rather than the dream I had, was the wisest decision I had made.

Just look at our two wonderful sons, who are our pride and joy. My darling boys — you have inherited a lot of your dad's beautiful virtues and don't you ever forget those qualities of your dad are important to display and sustain through life. You may not make your boss happy (being nice, kind and generous) but you would definitely make your wife and family happy. Believe me, there is nothing more important in life than your family.

So, let's all raise our glasses to wish this young man a very happy birthday and to continue his life's journey with God's blessings, longevity and prosperity, the three traditional Chinese Birthday wishes!

"Clarke" Family Portrait

1

PRELUDE

WAKING UP in the morning without having to check the time, other than out of curiosity — is it 7:30 a.m., 8:00 a.m. or 9:30 a.m.? In fact, I would challenge myself about whether I could sleep even longer. Knowing it is something I have no control over, no matter how hard I try, I quickly decide it is not worth worrying about anymore. Nonetheless, it is important to have a quick check of my Fitbit to see what score I have been awarded. If it is over eighty, the day would start with more enthusiasm and optimism, and if it is above my husband Peter's score, it would be even better.

After a quick wash, followed by the usual beauty routine which I have practised for decades, I would then wander leisurely downstairs to the kitchen. Whilst waiting for the kettle to boil, it is the perfect time to sort out the dishes in the dishwasher which has been working hard overnight. With just the two of us living at home, the dishwasher is now relatively easy to empty. If it were not for the extra hygiene I like, especially in pandemic times, I doubt it would be necessary to use it, since there is plenty of time to wash up.

Although the kitchen cupboard is packed with tea from China, many of the items are gifts from students or their parents and are of many different varieties, morning tea is always confined to an English brand, one of the many things I have been quite happy to adopt since moving to the UK. In fact, when we travel to Europe where more often coffee is the morning beverage, I would slip some tea bags into our suitcases.

We have a Victorian style spacious conservatory overlooking the back garden, with a birdbath and some bird seeds hanging on a feeding stand. Other than a small variety of English garden birds which come to visit us, I particularly enjoy watching the robin, or the bluetits washing themselves in the birdbath. Occasionally, we even have the pleasure of a short visit of a woodpecker which is something our neighbour feels a bit envious about. In addition, there is a family of black squirrels who like to jump between the garden fence and the garden shed. The day always begins well to see such lively activities in the garden under the sunshine in our conservatory with a cup of English tea in my hand.

Music has always been an important part of my life. It definitely feeds my soul and sets the day off really well. I would normally put on either some of Mozart's Sonatas or Schubert's Impromptus. This would help motivate me to do some practice later in the day too. I could not think of a better way to start the day enjoying a cup of English tea and listening either to Mitsuko Uchida playing Mozart or Alfred Brendel playing Schubert whilst looking out into our garden.

The Lunar New Year, the year of the Tiger, has slipped past quietly, again for the second year. Something I really miss at this time of the year is the Narcissus. This particular variety of Narcissus has a very sweet fragrance with small delicate white petals and bright yellow centres. When I lived in Hong Kong, my mother would normally display the carefully nurtured Narcissus bulbs in elegant Chinese porcelain pots and as they grew, the plants would be gently tied with a piece of shiny red ribbon and displayed on the sitting room's coffee table.

One of my friends gave me a box of Narcissus bulbs when we visited Hong Kong a few years ago. We carefully planted some in the garden on our return in the hope they would grow again the following year but sadly, they did not survive our cold winter. To make up for this loss, I was pleased to buy several Hyacinth bulbs from the Supermarket. After carefully replanting them in

larger pots, they blossomed beautifully and gave out a similar fragrance as the Chinese Narcissus. I am absolutely thrilled with the adaptation and how easily satisfied I was.

A few years ago, I did a major home redecoration, as this had not been done for over ten years. Whilst shopping for a new fireplace in an old Cambridge shop, I caught sight of a modern decorative metal oak tree wall hanger. The branches and leaves are very well balanced and they gave the appearance of a mature oak tree. It leads me to think that not only is it attractive on the wall above the fireplace, but more importantly, it is a symbol of what I have achieved. The branches and leaves are the sons I have raised as well as all the boys and girls I have looked after in my guardianship and summer school ventures. It was a fantastic fit above the fireplace, as if it was destined to live in my house.

At Christmas each year, I would tie some red Christmas balls on the branches, and to welcome Lunar New year I replaced them with little red decorative lanterns. This immediately created the Chinese New Year atmosphere in our sitting room. In addition, I bought some beautiful yellow/orange Chrysanthemums, another type of very popular flower in the Lunar New Year in China as they are a symbol of prosperity.

All over China, Lunar New Year, or the Spring Festival, is the most important event of the year, usually lasts about ten days. Businesses have to settle their debts before the arrival of the New Year. Companies always host an Annual Dinner for all the employees. Restaurants are generally booked at least two months in advance. It would be a banquet with eight dishes. Eight is an auspicious number to signal prosperity. Employees are given an extra month's salary as a bonus to thank them for their contribution.

On the domestic front, all homes were usually given a spring clean. My mother would prepare new clothes, new shoes and even new pyjamas for every child. With the help of our domestic helpers, she would make several New Year cakes. One of our favourites was made of mooli (a carrot-like vegetable but white and five times the size), dried shrimps, shallots, pork mixed with rice power and steamed afterwards for an hour. When I was young, there was no rice powder available and the rice mixture has to be made at home. The rice mixture is the binding ingredient and was therefore imperative.

We had a stone grinder, two round granite stones, a small one about ten inches in diameter on top of the bigger one which was about twice the diameter. After dinner each evening, my mother would start preparing the rice mixture with the domestic helper. She would carefully spoon some rice granules into a small hole (about an inch diameter) cut on the top stone. Then she would add a bit of water before the domestic helper turned the wooden handle at the top stone round and round until the rice water dripped out onto a drainer and into a sack tied below. The sacks of rice mixture would be left overnight to dry and turned into moist lumps of rice powder. It was a long and arduous process and normally took many, many hours with a great deal of determination and commitment. I think it was a labour of love.

I have been able to learn how to make this mooli cake from my mother, who in turn, learned from her mother. Before the Lunar New Year, I would follow the family tradition and make a few of these mooli cakes in the hope that the year ahead would bring us good fortune too.

When I was little, Hong Kong used to allow firecrackers on New Year's Eve and New Year's Day. Some families would worship their ancestors on New Year's Eve. They burned incense and left food in front of their ancestors' photos on a table usually placed in the corner of the sitting room. They believed their ancestors would continue to bless the family's fortunes if they

Stone rice mill – 1950

were remembered. As our family became Christians, we did not follow this tradition as we were meant only to worship God.

On New Year's day, we would start visiting our relatives and wish them Happy New Year. As children, we would receive a red packet (envelope) or two from them which would contain some lucky money inside. Our parents' red packets to us contained the biggest amount (usually twenty dollars, or two pounds). This was the most exciting part of the Lunar New Year for children. We would usually compare the amount inside the red packets between one relative and another. We were usually allowed to keep this money as our annual savings. Firecrackers were banned subsequently as they were perceived to be fire-hazards. Whilst walking on the pavements on our way to visit our relatives, I was terrified of some firecrackers being thrown into the streets by people living in the high-rise apartments. It was a great relief when the government imposed a ban on this tradition.

As our parents did not have any spare money to buy toys for their nine children, the lucky money gave us the opportunity. I remember I bought some paper dolls and cut out paper clothes made in the UK. I put them in an empty toffee box and kept all my paper dolls and clothes there. The box was my treasure for many years and was always next to my pillow.

As it happens, after a very busy and successful year in 2019, we were lucky enough to spend Christmas in Basel with our younger son and his wife. The first intimations of how serious the Corona Virus would become, were only known early in 2020. Beginning as an epidemic, it quickly turned into a pandemic.

The pandemic has turned the world upside down since it emerged in China in late 2019. I thought the Covid vaccine, so cleverly discovered by our scientists and so speedily available in the spring of the following year, would provide the solution to this pandemic and that it would be over in a year at the most. I quickly cancelled the marketing trip booked to Hong Kong in January and the 2020 Summer Programmes for students at Churchill College. I kept the 2021 booking with them, confident that we would re-open by then. This rather early cancellation surprised the College, as they thought we were deciding too soon and should wait a little longer. However, as my own maternal instincts, the sense of responsibility over children coming over from such a long way to our two-week Summer Programme from Australia, Hong Kong and China are rather strong, compared to

Oak tree sculpture in our drawing room at Chinese New Year

7

Relaxation: creating an Ikebana arrangement

some Western parents, I felt this was the correct decision. I was delighted to receive a call from the College several months later, to tell me that all their bookings for 2020 were cancelled following ours. In fact, I was consulted as to when I thought we would re-open up the Summer Programmes again. I told them that I would need to give our future more thought. There were several things on my mind, Covid's development, parents' confidence, economic impact on parents after the pandemic and the political situation. Would China be happy to send their students to UK's summer schools, after being criticised of their treatment of the Uyghurs? These thoughts continue to linger deep in my mind!

Little had I realised that the pandemic is rather more serious and complicated than I had ever imagined, as misinformation began circulating in the social media about the new vaccine and government mistakes were made. Successful countries like America became deeply divided and the pandemic has turned into a political game. We, here in the UK, although not as bad as in America, are also in a tricky position. Hong Kong, like China, adopted a "Dynamic Zero" tolerance policy to Covid. However, this has not prevented Omicron from slipping quietly in and it is spreading exponentially. Hong Kong is in a very serious situation due to the huge and dense population. I simply cannot see when our Summer Programme will re-open, in 2023 or beyond.

As such, with plenty of time on my hands, I decided not to

waste all these precious moments but to reflect on and record some valuable experiences in my life — 37 years of a mixed marriage, raising up a family without the support of my own family around, setting up and running Cambridge Guardians for 23 years where I looked after several hundred students from all over the world, and running Cambridge Programmes for fifteen years before the pandemic hit. More importantly, as our sons are half Chinese, I feel it is very important for them to know their heritage, and for their children's children too, where their Chinese heritage comes from.

2

EARLY LIFE IN HONG KONG

WITHOUT EXCEPTION, everyone who visits Hong Kong would be impressed by its success. In its 150 years under Great Britain's colonial rule, Hong Kong developed into one of the world's most successful financial centres and became a model on which today's China has built its many cities.

I always believe that Hong Kong was China's goose that laid the "golden eggs" which must be carefully preserved, even though the Communist Party at that time despised capitalism and considered it an evil ideology.

With hardly any natural resources, just a few acres of rice paddy fields, why was Hong Kong's progress and success much admired by countries all over the world and attracted millions of tourists every year? The reason is their most valuable resource: the millions of refugees who fled from the Japanese invasion of China between 1936 and 1945. My ancestors were amongst those refugees who came to Hong Kong by boat with no belongings.

My old school friend told me the story of how she, at the age of ten, came from Chiu Chow illegally by boat with her elder sister. Chiu Chow is a city in the eastern Guangdong province of China. It is located west of Fujian. She recalled hiding inside the bottom of a wooden boat which was carrying cargo from China to Hong Kong. She and the other illegal immigrants hid under a large piece of tarpaulin and sailed for two days in the dark.

There were marine patrol boats guarding the coastline of Hong Kong. As the boat sailed close to Hong Kong, the Captain would switch the lights off, tap hard on the tarpaulin to alert the illegal immigrants to remain silent until the marine boat moved away.

On arrival in Hong Kong, she recalled that the boat docked on the western point of Hong Kong. This is where large sacks of rice would be unloaded, piled up high, waiting for the coolies (unskilled labourers) to carry them on their shoulders to the shops. When night set in, she and the others would scramble out of the bottom of the boat, climbed over these rice sacks and ran into the city. She recalled her sister took her by tram to North Point where the rest of her family lived. Her family in China had left a few years before her and finally, she was re-united with them. She went to my old school, St Paul's Convent, to start her primary education and continued until she finished her secondary school.

She enjoyed a successful secretarial career with one of the largest shipping magnates in Hong Kong. She married an overseas Chinese professional from London and moved to the UK to continue her career with the Shipping magnate's family. She raised two sons who were very successful, one a banker with a top US bank in London while the other is a Legal Director of a large French company living in Paris. It is wonderful to see the success of immigrants like her who worked so hard with total dedication to her family.

My maiden name is "Hung", pronounced as "Ang" in the Fukian dialect, which means "abundant". This is a very common surname in this part of China. My father is one of the six children from his father's concubine (second wife). His family is from Fujian Province, South East China, facing the island of Taiwan. My paternal grandfather was a junior government official of the Qing Dynasty. His life span of sixty years between 1870 and

1930 encompassed some traumatic times in China including the Boxer Rebellion at the turn of the century and the end of the Qing Dynasty in 1911. There was what appeared to be an official photo of him in my grandmother's house, hanging on the wall in the sitting room. This looks like a Qing Dynasty official portrait photo. He had a pigtail and was wearing an attractively embroidered garment with a chain of beads. I recall my father told me that grandfather used to make frequent trips around China in his official duty, so he was not spending a huge amount of time at home with his family. Sadly, he could not recollect even one conversation between him and his father. In addition to his official ministerial role, he had a successful textile business which branched out to Hong Kong.

My paternal grandfather had a wife and a concubine who was my grandmother. Marriages in China were arranged by parents and children had no say in the matter. They had to accept whatever their parents had chosen for them, often without an initial meeting. Usually this would be between families of the same social and economic standing. There was a Chinese saying—"a bamboo door matches another bamboo door" (poor peasants usually live in houses with bamboo doors) and "a wooden door matches a wooden door" (wealthy households have double wooden doors which open towards you). Love in marriages never came into the picture.

I suspect parents were hoping that love would develop after

Grandfather in 1910

marriage was consummated. Sadly, it was often not the case. To make matters worse, if no male was produced by the wife, the husband's parents would then choose another girl, usually younger and may come from a slightly less well-off family (but not necessarily) to be a concubine.

Sometimes, the husband might meet a girl outside the family and fall in love with her. With his parents' permission, especially if there was no male heir, a second marital union would be gladly accepted. Sometimes, parents would be involved in choosing a concubine for their son. If the family was very wealthy they would find several girls (usually from poorer families in this case) and line them up for their son to choose. These young girls were paid a handsome sum and jewellery as dowry to the girl's family.

One would, therefore, expect that the marriage between a husband and his concubine would be happy and successful. Sadly, this often was not the case as human emotions such as jealousy from the wife would make the relationship between the concubine and her very, very difficult. You would hear stories of concubines being poisoned or thrown into the well in the Courtyard! Concubines had to be totally subservient to the wife. For example, she had to serve morning tea even though she did not need to prepare it. In the marriage ceremony, she would have to kneel down in front of the wife and pledge total obedience to her.

Having two wives brought huge disharmony in a family, contrary to the ancient belief—a large family is a sign of wealth and good fortune. I think the concept originally started when the woman in the family was unable to provide a son and heir.

This disharmony is reflected in my own ancestral home in China. In order to keep peace in the family, Grandfather decided to separate his wife and his concubine (my grandmother). My grandmother and her family were ordered to move to Hong Kong in about 1925. Number One wife and her family continued to stay in the family home in Xiamen. My grandmother had six sons and one daughter. My father was the fourth son. The mission for my grandmother was that she would keep an eye on grandfather's textile business and she would also be sent allowances from China.

According to my father, life wasn't too bad in Hong Kong when they first arrived. They lived in a three-storey tenement building. Grandmother and her favourite eldest son and his family lived on the top floor which has a balcony overlooking Pokfulam Road in the mid-levels. The other sons and their families all occupied a flat below each other. My parents were allocated the basement flat, in line with their seniority in the family — lowest!

Life started to change when Grandfather passed away in China in 1930. Naturally, the funds which used to arrive to support grandmother and her family were stopped by Wife Number One who gained control of the family fortune. The textile business in Hong Kong was quickly sold and no further funds were sent to Hong Kong.

The family would struggle to live if the sons did not start making a living independently quickly. My father and his brothers all got jobs and the family survived. My father worked as a bookkeeper and a rent collector for a wealthy Hong Kong businessman who owned many properties in addition to a cinema, called "Guo Tai", the same name as "Cathay Pacific" Airline.

Cathay Pacific Airway is the flag carrier of Hong Kong. The Airline's operations and subsidiaries have scheduled passenger and cargo services to more than 190 destinations in more than sixty countries worldwide. "Cathay" is the name by which North

China was known in Medieval Europe.

This was a special cinema which only showed films produced in China. I remember we were given coupons to the cinema from time to time as my father was a staff member. So, it was free for us to watch the films. The cinema showed some classical Chinese films which were of interest to my parents and they also showed some modern films made in Communist China. I remember a sense of pride when I showed the coupons to the man/woman guarding the entrance. However, going to this cinema, even with the privilege, was not something which I became addicted to at all. The reason is that they always started the film with propaganda from China — how glorious the Motherland is and how wonderful and happy are the people living under Communism, singing and dancing with a hoe in their hands. They were all wearing a dull grey uniform which didn't look too attractive, compared with the western style clothing we were wearing in Hong Kong. So, as children, we would rather go to see films from Hollywood or Disney. Thus the idea of Motherland China was something of which I was rather fearful!

After leaving the cinema, I would ask myself: if the people across the border from Hong Kong were so happy and the country was so glorious, why would the helper in our house often have to send parcels containing the old clothes and shoes that we children grew out of? Before winter arrived, my mother used to take me to the Chinese Emporium to buy some winter undergarments which were relatively cheap and would keep the many children in the family warm. Before we walked into the shop, Mum would always remind me not to say anything critical to the shopkeeper or I would be dragged away across the Border and be locked up for ever!

When I was young, I was aware that we had a big family with nine children, but it seemed very normal since my father

Example of Communist Chinese Propaganda Poster

came from a large family too. The family was so big that I never knew how many aunts and uncles I had as some of them lived in Xiamen and the Philippines.

I was aware that grandmother was the matriarch of the family. All her daughters-in-law had to "kow-tow" to her and they were treated like her maids. For example, on the first day of Chinese New Year, I saw my aunts kneel down to offer tea to grandmother, one by one. Her sons had to do the same. Then it was our turn although as children, we didn't have to kneel but just wished her, in a loud voice, "Happy New Year, Grandmother!".

Of the sons, the eldest, has the seniority and would normally inherit the family's assets. The wife of the eldest son was also in a powerful position, especially if her husband had a quiet and gentle personality.

If the family was not wealthy, then all the sons had to contribute part of their earnings to the family pot. Important family decisions such as marriages or investments were determined by grandmother or the eldest son or his wife.

I had to address each of my uncles and aunts by the position in the family. For instance, Number 6 Uncle and Number 6 Aunt. Other family members would address my father as Number 9 Uncle and my mother Number 9 Aunt.

Living so closely together in the same building did not bring harmony and happiness to anyone at all, from my observations at a young age. Knowing my mother's most junior rank in the household, she was exceedingly quiet and very pragmatic. She would not repeat to anyone anything she heard in case that got her or anyone else in trouble.

To pass the time, my paternal grandmother played mah-jong (a tile-based game with four players) regularly. She would either play with friends or her sons. Otherwise her daughters-in-law would have to play the game with her if none of these people was available.

My paternal grandmother was brought up in the Qing Dynasty where girls from a wealthy and respected family would have their feet bound from around the age of six. Hers were only three inches long which was the "gold" standard in those days. It must have been a real agony to be a girl born in a respectable family. Only girls from poor families who worked either in the fields or as domestic servants did not have their feet bound. So grandmother would wear beautifully embroidered tiny silk shoes. She had great difficulty walking and had to be supported whenever she needed to move about in the

Grandmother in 1910

17

house.

Every day, my Seventh Uncle's first wife, whom grandmother disliked because she was quiet and had no personality, had to put up with her foul temper especially when Grandmother lost in the game of Mah-jong. Grandmother would shout so loud that my mother could hear her voice in the basement of the building. Sometimes, grandmother would even throw the Mah-jong table over when she was in a rage. Every afternoon, my poor aunt had to massage her mother-in-law's poor legs for hours. This was probably because she was in pain all the time as she was unable to walk comfortably with such small bound feet. Once I witnessed my aunt untying grandmother's feet to wash them. I was shocked to see how ugly her feet were and they had a foul stench too! It must have been terrible for my poor aunt to have to do this every day. With grandmother's sanction, he married a second wife, from a dancing parlour and raised a family of seven with her. Years later, his second wife died of breast cancer. Being lonely on his own, Seventh Uncle looked up his first wife and I understand that they got back together and she was with him for several years before he passed away.

Sixth Uncle's wife was, however, the most valued and important member in the household. She controlled the purse strings, organised meals for grandmother and distributed the household duties.

Sixth Uncle was the intellectual in the house. He read Classical Chinese in Xiamen University and became a lecturer following his graduation. Sadly, he caught Tuberculosis and died at about the age of sixty, leaving a family of three children — two boys and a daughter.

Sixth Aunt was in mourning for years following her husband's death as she nursed him carefully during his illness. Apparently, she was one of his former students at university. She adored his intellect. He was a brilliant calligrapher and wrote poems. When I visited my aunt in the Care Home in her later life in Hong Kong, she showed me the book of poems that Sixth Uncle had written. She told me she kept this book under her pillow and she would read it every night before she went to sleep.

Jane was Sixth Aunt's only daughter whom I got to know in my later life, as she left Hong Kong at age of eighteen to sail to England to be trained as a nurse. I was under ten years old then. Jane was accepted to do her training in a women's hospital in East London, which no longer exists. One might think that as the only girl in the family, she would be spoiled. Unfortunately, that was the opposite in a Chinese family as girls were not valued at all. Jane loved my mother and she used to go to the basement and spent hours talking to her, probably voicing her feeling of being treated unfairly by her parents. The prejudice of favouring girls over boys had caused a major relationship breakdown with her mother. Sadly, Jane did not return to her home in Hong Kong to visit her mother for over forty years!

Jane went to St Clare's Girls' School, an English-speaking school run by Canadian Catholic nuns from Montreal. Many of the nuns spoke only French and limited English. Jane qualified as a Nurse after three years and then moved to work in the United States, presumably with much higher pay. At the time, as her father had passed away, she would have to send part of her income to support her mother and the family. My father liked Jane's English-speaking school (St Clare's Girls' School) and was of the opinion that because Hong Kong was a British Colony, his children must ALL learn English. However, he also felt that Chinese is a very important language, so he wanted all his children to start off their education in a Chinese-speaking school and afterwards in an English-speaking Secondary School. That was exactly what we did!

Ed was Sixth Aunt's youngest son, whom I got to know after I moved to the UK. After finishing his secondary school in Hong Kong, my aunt borrowed a year's College fees and sent Ed to The University in Toronto, Canada. There was only one university in Hong Kong at that time and it was almost impossible for anyone to get in unless you were the top scholar at school and lucky. Most wealthy parents would send their children to the UK, America, Canada or Australia for a university degree which was deemed to be the way to a successful future.

My cousin Ed chose to read Physics and Maths as these were his natural talents. He was, however, also talented in Drama. When I visited Ed's old school to promote my summer programme, Ed's Headmaster was still there and was in his final year. He remembered Ed well and told me that he was an "active" student, implying that he was good in the theatre and debating etc. and perhaps less interested to study hard, unlike most students in the school.

When Ed completed his degree in Canada, he was keen to do a Master's Degree followed by a PhD in Astrophysics and he had a dream of a career in science. However, his mother forbade him to pursue his dream as science is not a money-making career in Hong Kong. He, too, like Jane, had to send any income he made home to support the family. In fact, throughout Ed's studies in Canada, he had to work in his holidays. He told me one of his favourite summer jobs was collecting sandworms on the beaches. They were weighed in the shop and he was paid well compared with being a waiter in a Chinese Restaurant!

Knowing there was an education debt in Hong Kong to be repaid, Ed dutifully obeyed his mother's wish and decided to read Law in the end. With a good command of English, analytical ability and drama experience as well as debating whilst at school, Ed became a very successful lawyer in Toronto. His main interest was in Immigration and Criminal Law as Toronto has a large Chinese population who would need legal aid that Ed could provide especially in the field of immigration. He was right, he had lots of Chinese clients and quickly rose to become a partner in a short period of time. Due to his personal success, he decided to set up his own law firm. He also had a radio programme where he explained immigration law to the Chinese living in Canada. He was very well known by the Chinese community in Toronto. Sadly, Ed had Motor Neurone Disease in his sixties and decided to end his life in Switzerland, after failing to get successful treatment. Ed's only daughter, whom he adored, was just a teenager when he passed away. Like her father, she is also pursuing a career in Law.

Since money ran out in the family after grandfather passed away, my father had to seek employment at a relatively young age. He was educated at home when he was growing up in China by a Tutor when Grandfather was alive. He would learn about Confucius' teaching as well as the Chinese philosophers like Mencius and Zhuangzi. He recalled that his tutor was rather strict and if he slipped when he had to recite the Classical literature that he was taught, he would get a hard slap on his hand by the tutor.

My father died in Australia, aged 96, having migrated there thirty years earlier from Hong Kong. After arriving in an English-speaking country and rather than learning to speak English or Australian so he could integrate with the community, he chose to spend a lot of time in the library studying "Yi Jing", one of the oldest of Chinese classics. His love of learning never left him, perhaps because he was denied an education in his childhood which is a real tragedy.

My parents' marriage was arranged by my paternal Grandmother and my maternal Great-grandmother.

Grandmother often played Mah-jong with my maternal Great-grandmother and they became friends. Mum was barely 21 when the marriage was arranged for her. She was born in Cebu City in the Philippines. Her mother was from Xiamen and got married when she was only eighteen. I understand that my maternal Great-grandfather had a Spanish wife. So my mother was one-quarter Spanish and I have an eighth Spanish blood!

My maternal great-grandfather was already married in China before going out to the Philippines. As was very common in those days, people from Fujian province were very outward looking as the province is near the South China Sea. Many men from Fujian Province went to the Philippines, Singapore, Malaysia and Indonesia to trade and remitted money to support their families back in China. When I was little, my mother used to take us to visit grandmother and great-grandmother (who lived together in the same house) on Sundays and I recall trying out different snacks which were so exciting. These snacks came from exotic places in Southeast Asia and were brought to Hong Kong by our distant relatives. My grandmother's favourite beverage was actually Java coffee which is a very finely ground coffee powder, drunk with sugar and no milk, rather than Chinese tea. Perhaps with some mixed European blood in her, my mother's favourite beverage was also coffee, not tea.

Mum's maternal great-grandfather left his wife in China to live in the Philippines to trade and there, he fell in love with a lady, who originated from Spain which ruled the Philippines between 1565 and 1898. I understand that he dutifully sent money home to his first wife but never returned to visit her. One day, a letter arrived from China urging him to return to China to visit his wife who was seriously ill. Apparently, this was a ploy to make him return to China, as previous letters to ask him to return had fallen on deaf ears.

In order to find out the truth whether his wife in China was really ill, mum's paternal great-grandfather decided to send my grandmother, his daughter-in-law instead, to China. Indeed, his first wife was not ill at all. In fact, she was very angry that her own husband did not return to visit and comfort her but sent someone else! In her anger, she began to mistreat my grandmother. In fact, she even tried to poison her by putting something in her food. Luckily my grandmother just fell ill and recovered. Eventually, after staying for several upsetting months, she decided to return to the Philippines.

My mother sadly lost her father through sudden illness at the age of eight. Her childhood was completely shattered. She remembered having a short-lived but happy childhood in the Philippines. They lived in a large house and she recalled the shining wooden floor boards which were beautifully polished by the maids daily. She also enjoyed the lovely sweet mangoes from the trees in the garden. She very much enjoyed her schooling there and in particular the love and warmth of her father and the relatives around her.

After losing her husband, grandmother decided to bring her three relatively young children home to China, my mother (aged eight), her younger sister (aged six) and brother (aged two). They moved back to great-grandmother's home which was a very large house in the centre of Xiamen City. Great-grandmother had several sons and they were all successful in trade and enjoyed a comfortable living. Grandmother and her family were welcome to re-join the family. Mother recalled she had some joyful days and stability in China having lost her father. She still remembered very well the large Longan tree in the backyard. During August, when the fruits appeared, she would climb the tree to collect them. The longans were really juicy, she told me with joy on her face. She also had cousins to play with as they were living close by.

My paternal grandmother's brother ran an incense business in China. As many Chinese at that time worshipped Buddhas and ancestors, it was a prosperous trade. They apparently exported their products to Surabaya in Indonesia. My mother and her sisters helped package these sticks when they returned home from school. There were fifty sticks in each packet and the label had a Chinese girl wearing a straw hat and sandals. It was the "Three Rivers" brand.

Although mother never complained about life, I was aware that she had very little self-confidence. This is mainly because she was only a "guest" at her grandmother's home. The family was financially totally dependent on her grandmother and Uncles' support. In return for food, lodging and schooling for the children, my grandmother had to help with cooking in the house. I am sure my mother must have been told many times not to demand anything but to be grateful for everything she received.

It was only as I grew up and left home that I realised how clever my mother was even though she never had the opportunity of an education. Mum was excellent in problem solving. With a large family of nine children (four boys and five girls), she was quick to resolve difficulties. She was very organised so the home was always tidy. She was also extremely artistic. This was apparent when she took up Japanese flower arrangement called "Ikebana" and managed to graduate from the course at a teacher's level. It is probably the reason that I have also lately taken up "Ikebana" flower arrangement lessons, having found a Japanese lady in Cambridge who gives regular lessons.

My mother also had a great sense of colour and was always dressed beautifully in a Chinese style dress, called "cheongsam". Perhaps with a bit of her European heritage, she always had an open mind and was fond of the West. For example, she would

Chinese New Year with Parents in Hong Kong 1985

prefer eating western food than Chinese food and of course, her morning coffee!

Sadly, around the age of eighteen, my mother's life was disrupted the second time when the Japanese invaded China. One of her uncles decided that all the women in the house must leave immediately by boat to safety in Hong Kong. So, great-grandmother, grandmother and her children, accompanied by one of the uncles left Fujian to Hong Kong. My aunt, mother's younger sister, now in her nineties recalled how she climbed up the gangplank to the deck of the ship in great excitement on all fours!

On arrival in Hong Kong, Uncle rented a large apartment in the western district for the family to live. It was on the first floor, above a rice shop. I recall as a young child, my mother would take me to visit grandmother and great-grandmother regularly on Sundays. We had to climb up a flight of wooden stairs and

Mother's portrait at age eighteen

it was pitch black. I was terrified and had to climb very slowly holding my mother's hand, with my heart pounding as you couldn't see in front or up. Even today, I could still smell the rice grains as we walked past the large open buckets of different types of rice through the shop!

Great-grandmother's flat had three bedrooms on the left-hand side of a long corridor as you entered. The kitchen was located at the back of the house, where my grandmother spent most of the day. There was a lounge beyond the bedrooms. In the lounge was a set of old Chinese furniture. They were made of red rosewood with grey/white stone in the centre. There was a long seater, also made of the same kind of material, but with no cushions.

It was wonderful to see grandmother and great-grandmother once we entered the flat. They loved children and I recall Great-grandmother wanted me to sit with her in her bed. She, too, had tiny bound feet, like my paternal grandmother; so she usually

Four Generations
Figure 1 Back Row From left – Mother, Grandmother, Great-Grandmother and Father;
Rebecca on Front right

just sat on her bed all day, with meals brought to her room by her daughter. I thought her bed was a very high one and I had difficulty climbing on to it, most possibly because I was very small at the time.

Great-grandmother's bedroom had no windows. All the three bedrooms in the apartment had wooden basic partitions (about seven feet high and you had to step over a wooden beam into the bedrooms). Naturally, one could hear everyone's conversations and activities. Great-grandmother's bed had a straw mat (apparently it was of the best quality so she could be kept cool in the summer). It looked shiny and had a lovely pattern, brown and beige. She had a wooden pillow with a dent in the middle for her head to rest. The pillow had a shiny gloss which I believe is lacquer. Fujian is famous in making lacquer.

Grandmother was a chain smoker and mother and I spent

hours in her room, breathing in her cigarette smoke not knowing anything about passive smoking at that time. She would be talking about her son, her other daughter and other members of her family in Hong Kong and in other parts of South-east Asia.

Sunday afternoon visiting great-grandmother was always very joyful with lots of snacks, meals and listening to adults' gossip! These would include relatives who have gone to live in the Philippines or Indonesia. Occasionally, there were mah-jong games being played which at times were extremely annoying. It seemed to me at the time that it was going on forever even though I was extremely tired and wanted to go home to bed! In addition, I found the noise of the tiles very loud when one game ended and the players had to shuffle the tiles around and set up four walls to start the game again.

Mah-jong is quite a long game, even at a very early age, I learned that it is where lots of gossip took place and friendships formed. There would be laughter if the players got on with each other and you soon found out the different personalities of the players. Some would be aggressive and using tactics to stop other players from winning at the expense of not winning the game yourself. It could really be a game of challenging the opponents if the player is lucky to have the right tiles and engaging your brain in a very intense manner. Alternatively, one could easily lose the friendship of another player who doesn't lose well!

Looking back at my parents' life, I must marvel at their diplomacy living under the same household as grandmother and all the other members of my father's family. As I recall, no fight or quarrels ever took place which was absolutely incredible bearing in mind how ill-tempered grandmother was.

As our family grew, my parents moved out of the tenement building in West Point where my paternal grandmother and all the relations lived when I was about three years old. We moved to a rented flat in Happy Valley which was a very quiet, up and coming residential area. There were only two bedrooms and up to now, I cannot remember how my parents could have squeezed so many children into the flat in addition to a domestic helper!

Originally, the name Happy Valley derives from a desire by British soldiers in 1840 to combat its dreaded reputation as a malaria-infested swamp. Their tombstones are still evident in the Happy Valley cemetery. It is now famous as the location for its superb race- course where horse races take place every weekend. Over 100 years ago, I heard that the local residents were not allowed to watch the race. It was only for the Colonial British. Local people stood on a huge rock on the hillside so they could watch the races. The racecourse is owned by The Jockey Club, founded in 1884. In 1959, it was granted a Royal Charter and renamed The Royal Hong Kong Jockey Club. The institution reverted to is original name in 1996 due to the transfer of sovereignty of Hong Kong in 1997. The Jockey Club has an annual revenue of 36 billion US dollars.

We lived on the third floor on a side street off the main road up the hill. My father sent me and all my sisters to a Catholic Chinese School up the road, called Precious Blood School. It has a Kindergarten section as well as a Primary school and is run by some Chinese Catholic nuns.

All lessons were conducted in Chinese and it was hard learning the language. Reading means you have to learn to recognise each Chinese character and that involves writing and memorising each character. At about age eight, we had to use a Chinese brush and dip it in black ink to write Chinese characters. There was a template placed between two sheets of thin paper. Holding a Chinese brush is not like holding a pencil. One has to grip the pen with just the thumb and the index finger. The pen has to be held up perpendicularly! This was an exercise we had to do at least once a week. What was also difficult is that in order to learn the characters, the teacher needed to give us dictation regularly. The night before dictation, if my father came home late from work and I had already gone to bed, he would wake me up to do dictation with him!

Starting in kindergarten at age four, we had to learn to write our Chinese names, which consist of three characters. Depending on which characters your parents choose, this was also very tricky. My Chinese name has thirty-five strokes which is a lot for a child of four to remember. My younger sister has a name with forty-two strokes and I recalled she used to get into trouble with my father who was so cross that she couldn't write her name! The names have very special meanings. My name means "an elegant, good and refined person to be praised or admired".

I enjoyed music lessons especially at school. One day, the music teacher told me to let my mother know that I am 'musical'. I didn't understand, at age four, what that meant and told my mother when I went home anyway. As time passed, my love of music, especially the piano, has grown even more, especially when the new neighbour next door had a daughter who played the piano. Every evening when she started to practise, I would put my head near the wall to the flat next door so I could hear it better. I particularly enjoyed her Chopin nocturnes.

I do not recall that we were given any toys to play with when I was growing up in that small flat in Happy Valley. We noticed there were children in the flat opposite us. One day, we spotted a very bright round image on the ceiling. Looking out from our bedroom window, we realised that the young boy across the road was shining a mirror into our room. Quickly we responded with our own mirror and that was a rather exciting mirror fight in the afternoon.

Another excitement was occasional monkey show on the

street. One day, we heard a man banging a gong quite loudly in the street. We all rushed to see what was going on in the street below from our bedroom window. There we saw a man with a monkey on his shoulder and a long wooden pole which he placed over his other shoulder. The monkey had a rope tied to his master. Upon instructions from his master, the monkey would perform tricks. One I remember vividly was swinging the monkey round the top of the pole at a fast speed! After the show ended, the man would hold out his cap and asked the residents to throw some coins to him which we did. In return, he would throw a piece of wrapped up preserved olive through the window. A very sad incident happened one day. The monkey managed to slip off the rope and jumped onto the telegraph pole. After long negotiations, the monkey still refused his master's order to come back to him. He now played tricks with his master by jumping down to the road and quickly up the telegraph pole. Sadly, in the end, the monkey was electrocuted. It was very upsetting to watch the end of this monkey.

In addition to his regular office job, my father bought a fishing junk. He also hired a local fisherman to catch fish for him and sell them to the wholesale fish market in Aberdeen to increase the family income. Fish is considered an especially healthy food and is in strong demand. Sometimes, when the catch was very successful, the fisherman would bring us the surplus and there would be many enormous fish including garoupas which was, at the time, one of the expensive types. At times, we had so many fish that mum converted the fresh fish into a "fish floss", a light and fluffy texture similar to candy floss. It is usually used as a topping for many foods, such as congee (rice porridge).

As Hong Kong's climate is subtropical, typhoons usually hit the territory between July and September. This naturally had a negative impact on the fishing trade for three months of the year.

I remember listening to my father's anxious voice speaking to the fisherman on the telephone before and after the storm. In addition, there were maintenance problems on the junk which seemed to trouble him.

The additional income my father was able to make certainly brought benefits as he was able to buy a flat, for the first time in 1957. It was a brand-new twelve storey flat located in Happy Valley, facing the Jockey Club Racecourse. In fact, it was the first high rise building on the road around the racetrack. We were on the eighth floor so my father could go out to the balcony to watch the weekly races and put a bet on them!

It was very exciting moving into a high rise from the small third storey flat we occupied before. At the beginning, I used to be woken up every morning, at around 6:00 am, by the sound of the horses trotting down from the stables half-way up the hill to the racetrack led by their grooms. As more buildings were built and traffic began to build up in the area, the sound of the horses didn't seem to have any effect on my sleep.

My youngest brother was born soon after we moved into the new flat which had three bedrooms. We now had nine children living there — four boys and five girls of whom I was the eldest of the girls and number three in the family. I had two older brothers in front of me and two youngest brothers after my youngest sister. It is understandable why a bigger flat was necessary. In addition, my mother hired two domestic helpers. One of them worked in the kitchen, did all the shopping, and cooked the meals. The other one helped with the children.

As our family grew, it was inevitable that the family needed more domestic help from when I was about four or five years old. It wasn't particularly expensive, and my recollection was that they cost about HK$70 per month (£7). Then the cost rose to about HK$120 per month (£12) by the time the children all grew

Family of nine children (aged from 2 to 13 years old)

up and help wasn't as essential. The reason it was so inexpensive was that there were lots of unskilled labourers available, as they had fled Communist China to Hong Kong and were allowed to stay.

I was particularly attached to one of the helpers whom I would claim as my own "nanny". I believe she was also extremely fond of me to the extent that my grandmother who came to visit us from time to time, asked Nanny why she would carry me on her back whilst she would hold my younger sister's hand and made her walk when we went out.

Nanny was a young widow, barely in her early thirties, when she fled China to come to Hong Kong to work as a domestic helper after the death of her husband. She had a young son whom she was unable to bring with her. He was left behind in China under someone else's care. Nanny would send money back to China regularly to support her son.

Nanny was illiterate and I remember she would take me with

her whenever she needed to go to a scribe who would help her write letters to her son. When a letter arrived for Nanny, I would take the letter, held upside down, as I was unable to read at the tender age of three, and made up an imaginary story to tell her. It would usually make her laugh as I would tell her that her son loves her very much and when he grows up, he would earn a lot of money and give it all to her so she wouldn't have to work so hard anymore!

I was overjoyed one day when I heard that my father was able to find an engineering apprenticeship for Nanny's son called "Ah Wor", which when joined with another character meant "peace". With the possibility of a job, Ah Wor could now make an application to travel to Hong Kong which he did. Unfortunately, after Ah Wor was qualified as an engineer, Nanny quit working for us. I know Nanny was terribly grateful to my father for organising this opportunity for her son.

I kept in touch with Nanny for many years to come and would visit her when I had a chance to travel to Hong Kong. One year when I came to see Nanny, I was very upset to learn that Ah Wor has contracted cancer in the stomach. Sadly, he died in his forties, leaving his wife and three relatively young children. When I visited Ah Wor in the hospital before he passed away, he remained calm and cheerful even knowing he had not got long to live. He expressed to me how grateful he was to my father for letting him be reunited with his mother in Hong Kong with this wonderful apprenticeship which changed his life!

Soon after her son's death, Nanny started working as a domestic helper again so that she could help with the finances of her son's young family. She gave them every penny she had until her youngest grand-daughter graduated from University and all her three grandchildren had jobs. Nanny worked until she was over seventy as a domestic helper and when she retired, she was offered a unit under the government's Public Housing Scheme. This had only one room, probably three-by-three metres, a small toilet and a tiny cooking area. She lived there for several years until her mobility became a problem. Sadly, her daughter-in-law felt she had to arrange for her to live in a Care Home. Nanny was always cheerful when I visited her in her over-crowded Care Home. Her food had to be ground up although she was able to feed herself but she had great difficulty walking. Nonetheless, she never complained and was very proud to introduce me to other elderly residents whose beds were near hers. When I got married, Nanny gave me a gold bracelet, which is one of my greatest treasures.

Nanny at her grandson's graduation

3

SCHOOLDAYS IN HONG KONG

WHEN I turned ten, my father decided that all his daughters must follow our cousin Jane's footsteps and join her old English-speaking School, called St Clare's Primary School in Bonham Road, Mid-Levels. Having studied in a Chinese Primary School up to then, the transition was known to be rather tricky as I hardly knew much English. In the Chinese primary school which I had been attending, all lessons were taught in Chinese except perhaps one or two English lessons a week. However, I don't seem to remember any difficulties involved moving school or fitting into the new school where all the lessons were taught in English. In fact, I was quietly pleased that my father did not have to wake me up from my sleep in the evening to do any more Chinese dictation with him!

One other great transformation in attending St Clare's Primary School was that I found a nun there, Sister Lucille, who gave piano lessons to students. That was an exciting find as I was always keen to take up piano lessons, having heard my next-door neighbour practising. Naturally that involved extra cost and that was something I needed to negotiate with my father. The usual way of approaching him for money was through my mother because my father was very much like a Victorian one who was quite distant and could get into a bit of a temper without any warning as I witnessed some of the quarrels he had with my mother. They were usually about money too! The immediate reaction of my father about piano lessons was that our home was very small and with so many children, there wasn't any space to put a piano in nor could he afford to buy one. In reply to his comments, I told my mother to relay to my father that there was no need to buy me a piano as the primary school had lots of music practice rooms. Actually I exaggerated a little, there was only one music practice room. The cost of the piano lessons was the equivalent of three pounds-a-month and there was no charge for using the school's practice room. After lots of discussion, my mother told my father that the music teacher had told her when I was in the kindergarten that I was musical. In the end, my mother won the argument and he finally agreed that I could start piano lessons! Asking for piano lesson fees was always extremely painful. When I turned fourteen and my English had greatly improved, I began to tutor a neighbour's son, aged eleven, in English so I could eventually stop asking my father to fund my piano lessons. This actually has had an impact on my view on life as I began to realise that financial independence was vital. I also noticed how terrible it was for my mother who also had to keep asking for her monthly housekeeping allowance.

The piano lessons with the nun were quite tense and stressful, at the best of times. The main reason was that Sister Lucille did not speak much English. Her native tongue was Canadian French as she came from Quebec. It was quite difficult to understand her, but I managed to learn to read music. Every morning, I had to get up quite early to catch the bus from Happy Valley to Central. Then I had to change bus from Central to Mid-Levels and arrived at 7:30 a.m. so that I could start my piano practice. The journey alone would take up to 45 minutes.

Sister Lucille took her students very seriously and asked us to

First piano lesson with Sister Lucille

play in concerts regularly and definitely before Christmas. She taught us the Royal College of Music Exam Syllabus and I did reasonably well. One day, Sister Lucille got into a bad temper whilst teaching me as she was probably tired at the end of the day. Out of the blue, she slapped hard on my arm and made me jump. I was not even aware of what I did wrong as I always tried hard and never missed my morning practice. Perhaps I did not understand her "pidgin" English and this upset her.

I was really upset, angry and shocked as her slap was quite hard that I shed some tears after I left her room. When I arrived home, I told my mother that I did not wish to continue with my piano lessons anymore. This was probably a year or so after I started lessons with Sister Lucille. I did not recall if my mother asked me for the reason but what I remember very well was her response: your father said that your interest in piano lessons wouldn't last! I was terribly annoyed when I heard this and immediately changed my mind. The following morning, I travelled to school at the usual time and started my practice at 7:30 a.m. as usual. Sister Lucille heard my playing and came in to the room and gave me a big hug and a tight squeeze. She was always very temperamental, and all her students had to put up with her tantrums! To this day, I still hate the French language as this reminds me of Sister Lucille who would always speak in French when she was in a bad mood, very swiftly and expressively and furthermore, I did not understand a word!

My greatest improvement on the piano front was when Sister Lucille was relocated back to the Headquarters of the Convent in Canada. I shall always be grateful for the arrangements she made for a few of her senior students (of whom I was pleased to be included) to be introduced to a brilliant piano teacher she knew, Mrs Marie Ribeiro.

Mrs Ribeiro is Portuguese and her family originated from Macau. This is a very small island near Hong Kong which was ruled by Portugal from 1557 to 1999. The main economy of Macau is the casino business. Mrs Ribeiro lived with her husband and three teenage sons in a beautiful house in Deep Water Bay. It was exceptionally unusual for anyone to live in a "house" in Hong Kong except multi-millionaires or expatriates from large trading firms such as Jardines or Swires or Hongkong and Shanghai Bank. In fact, this was the first house I had ever visited. Mrs Ribeiro's family must have accumulated some wealth over the decades. To have piano lessons with Mrs Ribeiro was a really exciting and

My inspirational piano teacher, Mrs Ribeiro and Cecilia

enjoyable experience. After getting off the bus, there was a small path by the side of the road which led down the hill to her house. It was like a secret passage! As we approached the house, there would always be piano music flowing and I could often hear the music until we arrived at the front door. It was just magical and I felt really blessed to have this opportunity. Because Mrs Ribeiro was a busy teacher, I was only given a lesson once a month but that was worth waiting for.

Under Mrs Ribeiro, my piano playing improved greatly. She gave me lots of encouragement and her teaching was so clear and easy to understand. I was definitely on an upward musical journey with her. Because of this, I put a lot of practice in every day and really looked forward to every lesson she was able to offer.

There was an annual schools' Speech and Music Festival in Hong Kong which was a fierce competition amongst schools. Newspapers liked to publish results every day and parents took the results very seriously. This Festival was always a battle ground for schools and parents took note as to the names of the winning schools. The aim was that they would send their children there when opportunities arose. In Hong Kong, the names of the schools were so very important and parents assumed that their children would automatically do better if they studied there!

Adjudicators of the Festival came from The Royal College of Music and some of the top London Drama Schools. There were usually hundreds of different competitions including all types of musical instruments and school orchestras. Mrs Ribeiro suggested I entered some of the competitions on offer. I felt it was quite ambitious as I didn't think I was good enough although I had improved since the days of Sister Lucille. Anyway, I did not wish to disappoint Mrs Ribeiro who gave me a bit more of her time to prepare me for the competition. I was in two separate competitions: Mozart sonatas and Chopin waltzes.

There were more than a hundred competitors in each of these classes. I was very nervous as I went to the venue on my own. I told myself I should just enjoy my piece and do my very best. After the competition in the Mozart Sonata Class, the adjudicator took a much longer time than usual to announce the top three winners. He explained to the audience when he came on to the stage that it was a tough one to choose between the first and the second prize winners. In the end he made the choice on the premise that the second prize winner played with the music in front. Then I heard my name announced after the first prize winner — I was in total shock. The winner of the Class was called Melody Wu. She has been getting lots of prizes in the festival, so it was amazing that I could be just behind her in this particular class!

In the second competition which I entered and played one of Chopin's waltzes — I came third which, again, was a total surprise. One of the reasons was that I did not expect to win at all and went in to enjoy playing the piece as Chopin was my favourite composer.

After leaving St. Clare's Primary School, I joined their newly built Senior School on Mount Davis Road. This was a new site and was terribly remote, with hardly any houses around. It was even longer for me to travel from home to school every day. I had to change bus, not once but twice and it took over an hour.

The school had no canteen or kitchen so we would have to bring our own lunches. My lunch (rice and some meat and vegetables) was usually prepared by our domestic helper and put in a warm flask. By the time I opened the flask at lunch time, many hours since the food was prepared, it had gone cold and did not taste nice at all. Usually, I took a look and disliked the smell it gave. I closed the lid again and took the flask home. My health took a dip for not eating all day and it was noticeable that I did not grow much at a time when children of my age should be eating massive amounts.

My domestic helper informed my mother who was beginning to feel worried. So after one year and a term in the secondary school, I left to join St Paul's Convent School which is a fifteen-to-twenty minute walk from home. I chose this school because my friend who had piano lessons with Sister Lucille went there. It had an excellent reputation and I particularly liked their uniform. It was a white blouse, buttoned at the back and a skirt with a tartan pattern. The junior girls had a bow tie worn under the collar of the blouse and the secondary school girls worn a tartan patterned tie. The most distinguishing feature about the uniform was that every girl must wear "black and white" shoes with laces.

The girls at St Paul's were very different from those at St Clare's. They all seemed terribly confident in themselves. They were very active in extra-curricular activities and there were many clubs and societies. Each club or society had a little badge to represent it. So, if you joined many societies, your tie was

Summer uniform

loaded with badges!

St Paul's Convent School was also run by nuns and they were from a French Catholic Order from Chartres although none of the nuns there was French. The Headmistress was, in fact, Irish, and was very strict. No one was allowed to be heard speaking any language other than English around the school.

Winter uniform

Music was also an important part of school life, bearing in mind the importance of the Annual Music Festival. The School, therefore, had a very strong choir run by a Filipino nun. As I joined late, I was unable to be involved in this part of school life, although I would have loved to. On one occasion, I thought my opportunity had come. There was a school concert and I put my name down. I was planning to play my Mozart sonata in which I had done well at the Music Festival before. On the day of the concert, I discovered that this Filipino nun had not included my performance. The worst thing was that she did not even notice. I was terribly upset and disappointed, but I knew there was no point challenging her. As she brought glory to the school by winning many competitions in the music festival, other than the Headmistress, she was the most powerful nun in the school. She was well aware of this.

As I joined the school in the middle of an academic year, the transition was difficult, especially in a competitive girls' school.

43

I had a desk which was put alongside the usually two joined up desks. This made me stand out in class especially when the teacher wanted to ask a question. Classes were relatively big, about 36 and I was number 37!

Although I had a friend before I joined the school, I was not in her class. She was in Class C. I was in Class B, which had a higher academic standard. Class A had students who were not native Hong Kong residents and they did not do Chinese subjects whereas the rest of the year group all had to do one or two Chinese subjects. So I was put in a class with generally smart girls around. It was very uncomfortable for the rest of the two terms having to sit in such an eye-catching seat. I put my head into my studies even more as I knew I could be quizzed by any teacher who came in and the rest of the girls were all watching the performance of this "new arrival". It was naturally impossible to make friends in the class as they all had their own friendship groups. During break time, I would normally mingle with my old friend and her group of friends in the playground.

At the end of the first year at the school, I came seventh out of the class of 37. I was quite relieved and felt I was beginning to be accepted by the girls in my Form, although my loyalty was still with my friend next door. I also formed a good friendship with the girls in Class C, too.

As I was unable to be involved in the School Choir or any other musical activities in the school, I joined the Legion of Mary which, in fact, has had an important impact on my life. As a result of my brother's influence in the local Catholic Church, the whole family became Catholics whilst I was still in the First Form of St Clare's Secondary School.

The Legion of Mary is a Catholic Society which met once a week. We had a Spiritual Director and that was our Headmistress, Sister Rose. A Senior girl was the President and there was a Secretary who took minutes. We usually started the meeting with a Prayer and Sister Rose was always in attendance. We were given assignments each week after the meeting. The assignments were undertaken by two members. It would involve visiting patients in the local hospitals, visiting lonely adults at their homes or visiting families who lived up the hillside by our school in wooden huts.

Wooden huts were terribly unsafe places and there were hundreds up the side of the hill near our school. There was no running water inside the hut. Water was from a mains tap outside and water had to be carried into the hut for cooking or bathing. There was a stream coming down the hillside and people would bring their detergents and wash their clothing on the rocks by the stream.

There was a huge fire which burned down a shanty town, Shek Kip Mei, of immigrants from China who fled to Hong Kong on December 25, 1953. A total of 53,000 people were made homeless. This was started when a bucket of molten rubber was knocked onto a kerosene stove inside a squatter hut.

I was assigned to a girl, aged twelve called "Chung Kit-Ching". I was a couple of years older than her. She lived in the wooden hut with her parents and her two younger brothers. Her parents both went to work and she had to look after her younger brothers. My assignment was to visit her and teach her the Catechism. Kit-Ching's father was a tailor. He made Chinese-style men's jackets. Her mother worked in a plastic flower factory. Kit-Ching did not even have the opportunity to finish her Primary School education before she was given the role of child minding on her two younger brothers, aged four and six.

Following my weekly visits to the huts to see Kit-Ching, as a teenager of fourteen or fifteen years old, I felt so lucky that I could go to school and had a warm bed even though the flat was always crowded with siblings and visiting relatives. I had to share the top of a bunk bed with another sister. Bunk beds were the only way my parents could house so many children in a three-bedroom flat!

Finding a quiet place to study at home was a challenge. There was only one Library in Hong Kong and it was where you borrowed books. It was not a place where you could sit and study as libraries here in the UK are. The flat had a balcony and that was where I could get away from the noise in the house. I usually sat at the end of the balcony to study or if the weather was poor, I would go to the domestic helper's tiny room at the back of the kitchen and sat on her bed with my books. When I had finished my studies, sometimes I would turn on her radio and listen to "Sherlock Holmes" which I found exciting and fascinating. It was all translated into Cantonese, the local language. It was a great end for my day! Years later, I was so excited to be invited to dine at the Sherlock Holmes Restaurant on Baker Street by the Registrar of Pitman's Central College where I worked.

With my help and guidance, Kit-Ching was eventually baptised into the Catholic Church, to the Headmistress' delight. I got the impression from her that I had rescued a soul! I became Kit-Ching's God-mother, even though I was only a few years older than she. I saw Kit-Ching regularly even after I had left school. She addressed me as her "sister", even to this day. We both felt this title was more appropriate for our relationship.

In addition to the plastic flower industry which sprung up in Hong Kong in the early 1960's, the clothing industry took advantage of the relatively cheap, skilful and hard-working labour supply in Hong Kong. Without an education, Kit-Ching joined a garment factory. It was very common in those days if one has had no education. She worked her way up from an apprentice to a supervisor. She sat behind a sewing machine and worked ten hours a day, six or even sometimes seven days a week (if there were urgent consignments). She was very good with her hands. I was convinced that she had inherited her father's talent in tailoring. Several years later, she and a friend formed a business partnership. They became an independent contractor. When factories received large orders from abroad and were unable to manufacture the garments within their own factory capacity, they would send the order out to contractors like Kit-Ching and her business partner. Kit-Ching was thus able to increase her income substantially through immense hard work and commitment to success, working "24/7" for several years. I was extremely impressed when she told me she was able to buy two apartments, one after another, in Kowloon, close to the industrial area where she worked in a matter of five years.

After owning her own property, she and her family (parents and two brothers) moved out of government housing. "Ah Keung", meaning "strong", the older of the two brothers, became a bus driver. This was a relatively low paid job and it was therefore impossible for him to buy a property when he got married. Property prices in Hong Kong were very high and mortgages were not really available to working-class people. The deposit was usually around 30% of the purchase price. So Kit-Ching shared her apartment with Ah Keung and his family.

When the youngest brother got married and needed somewhere to live, Kit-Ching was able to put down a deposit so she could buy her second apartment and lease it to him. Working as a postman, there was no way her youngest brother could buy a property either. Four years ago, I was very impressed to hear that Kit-Ching used her own savings to finance one of her nieces to study Engineering in Swansea. This is absolutely an amazing success story of someone who was born into poverty but determined to find hope and helped the next generation to succeed.

In the 1980's, when Shenzhen was declared the first special economic zone by Deng Xiaoping, the effective leader of the Communist Party, there was a massive migration of labour from rural China. These workers were mobilised to develop this former quiet fishing village. From a manufacturing centre of garments and electronics, Shenzhen has now developed into the high-tech manufacturing centre in southern China today. Industrialists in Hong Kong began to move their factories across the border to take advantage of the cheap labour. Hong Kong became a very successful financial centre with a thriving tourism trade. Their property prices were amongst the highest in the world.

Because of Shenzhen's development, Kit-Ching lost her garment contracting business, as she was unable to beat the competition in China with exceedingly cheap labour. Yet, she would not give up fighting for survival. She applied and was successful in getting a job in a government hospital, working as a carer in the Men's geriatric unit. Once again, this was a very hard and rather difficult job. She had to feed the elderly, clean and wash them. The majority of these patients had no visitors. Kit-Ching was very kind and befriended them. At times, she even had to help the nurses clean up dead patients before they were moved to the hospital mortuary. In Hong Kong, staff performing this kind of work in the hospitals are labelled as "Ah Sum", meaning hospital maids. It is also relatively low-paid but the workers are entitled to a pension. Kit-Ching worked there until she retired at the age of 60. However, she stayed on as an Ah Sum working on just a daily wage but with no other benefits.

When I returned to visit her and her mother in Hong Kong a few years ago, I learned of an even darker side to their lives. Kit-Ching's mother was sold as a teenager to a spinster by her parents. She had to do the domestic chores for this lady and was

Kit-Ching and her family

generally kept as her companion. When the Japanese invaded China in the late 1930's, the spinster told her to run away as she was worried about her safety. Japanese soldiers were known to kill ruthlessly and also rape young girls. She was packed up with basic clothing and food and told to run south to Hong Kong, which was a British territory. She remembered running tirelessly as she heard gun shots behind her. When it got dark, she hid in a cemetery. She told me she felt bullets were flying over her head as she hid behind a tombstone!

Kit-Ching's mother met her future husband and they were married in Hong Kong. She told me that when she was born, her mother tried to sell her as she felt they could not afford to raise a child. Apparently, her mother has not discussed this idea with her father. The price her mother received for selling the infant Kit-Ching was only five Hong Kong Dollars (50 pence). Kit-Ching's father returned home in the evening and was shocked and angry that his wife has sold his daughter without consultation! He

49

demanded to know the people to whom she had sold the baby and that same evening, he went to bring Kit-Ching back home. It was terribly sad when they told me these two individuals' stories and I wondered whether the mother's own sale by her parents when she was young has transcended to her selling her own daughter or was it an issue of gender? In those days, sons were much more highly regarded than daughters. Not only were sons stronger in the fields producing family income but they remained with the family after marriage. Daughters, however, left the family to join their husband's own family, so were often regarded as a liability, hence occasionally sold off. As it turned out, of her three children, one girl and two boys, it is Kit-Ching, the daughter who was the main bread-winner of the family and now has provided two apartments for them to live!

The Japanese invasion of China reminded me of my mother's own story when she and her sister were living with my great-grandmother in Hong Kong. The Japanese occupied Hong Kong between 1941 and 1945. My father once told me that he had to bow whenever he came across a Japanese soldier in the street. If his bow wasn't low enough, he would get a kick in the face!

Japanese soldiers would knock at the residents' doors from time to time and asked to see if there were any young girls living there. They were usually raped if there were. My mother recalled how she and her sister had to hide under their mother's bed and rubbed their faces with charcoal, so they weren't easily visible.

From time to time, soldiers would knock at the doors of all the residents and demanded they came out to the street. The soldiers wanted to demonstrate to the residents what punishment they would get if they stole food. The victim's hands were tied back and he was shot dead by the Japanese soldier in front of the public. After the public execution, the residents were told to return to their homes.

My mother turned twenty-one during the Japanese occupation. One day, she was told to get married as her grandmother had found a suitable family for her. Although my mother had never met my father before, she trusted her family's choice. More importantly, she felt that since food was short, there would be one less mouth to feed in grandmother's house. She, therefore, dared not challenge her grandmother and mother's wish.

Married life was not easy, as I mentioned earlier, living under the same roof as my paternal grandmother. During the Japanese occupation, food was rationed. My mother recalled how my father weighed the rice daily for her to cook. I wondered whether because of lack of nutrition, my oldest brother was born with a club foot and hand.

Having large families was quite common when I was growing up. Most families had between five to seven children. Although infant mortality rate was low, Chinese preferred sons to daughters as males carried the family name. It was, therefore, normal for the assets of a family to be passed down only to the eldest son of the family. A good example was our next-door neighbour. They had seven children (two sons and five girls). The family was originally from Macau. They owned a small oyster farm. One day, they were cooking oysters and by accident, had left the oysters burning. Instead of throwing away the oysters, they decided to taste the over-cooked oysters and thought it would make a good sauce. That was the birth of the famous oyster sauce which is heavily utilised in the Chinese cuisine world-wide to this day.

This small oyster business turned into a multimillion-dollar trade and it was all in the hands of the eldest son. The girls had to help whilst the business was developing but they were not entitled to any of it. The youngest son, with the help of lawyers, managed to get a small settlement out of Court.

I always thought my father preferred sons to daughters. He had two sons followed by me and my four younger sisters. Then my two younger brothers came along and he was happy to finish the size of the family.

My eldest brother Frank was sent to college in America. I recall my mother explained to me that because of his club foot and hand, it would be important for him to be properly educated so that he would be able to support his family in future. It made total sense.

My second eldest brother Alex was regarded by my father as his smartest son. He didn't want to pursue further education after completing his secondary school and instead, he joined Hongkong and Shanghai Bank to be trained as a Programmer. It was a job with a good future as HSBC was probably the first bank in Hong Kong to be computerised. He did extremely well there and moved on to work for Tung Chee-Hwa's shipping company. Mr Tung later became the first Chief Executive of Hong Kong after Britain handed over Hong Kong to China.

As I was about to complete my secondary school, I was very keen to study music in England. My passion was in piano playing and I thought I might make a good piano teacher, like Mrs Ribeiro who really inspired me! I asked my mother to check if my father would be able to finance my ambition. This time, my father put his foot down about my desire to pursue music further. I remember after I returned home from the piano competitions and having done well, he did not make any comments. The next day, my name and photo was in the local newspaper and still, he said nothing. Instead, he told my mother that he would like me to be a school teacher. There was a teacher training College in Hong Kong, although fairly new at the time, called Northcote Training College. The College was named after one of the Governors of Hong Kong. My father told me that I should apply for a place after completing my secondary school education. He said that I could teach music too without going to a music college. As he didn't appreciate music, I was sure he didn't understand me at all. I also believe that he thought teaching would make a good profession for girls and that it was wrong of a girl like me to have any other ambitions. I was so angry with his remarks and plan for my future, I confronted him and asked him to explain why he had had so many children if he couldn't afford to educate them properly. He was apoplectic with rage and could not utter a word! I stormed back to my room after this episode.

I was not particularly impressed by any of my teachers at my school, so the idea of training to become a teacher was not appealing at all. Besides, many of my classmates were going abroad to UK Universities or American Colleges. Hong Kong had one and only one university and there was zero chance I could get in.

I had particularly frustrating and nasty experiences with two of the teachers. One of them was a nun who taught us Religious Studies. We were studying St Mark's Gospel, which was part of the exam syllabus. The method we used to learn was to recite the Gospel chapter by chapter, verse by verse. During lessons, Sister would randomly point to one of the girls who had to stand up and recite following the previous girl. My friend, Cynthia, found this so terrifying that she wet herself. At the end of the RS lesson, she would start to learn the following chapter in the playground in an attempt to push every sentence into her brain. I felt very sorry for her even though, at each lesson with this nun, my own heart was beating fast and I always breathed a sigh of relief when the bell rang! Another teacher whom I found impossible to learn from was the Maths teacher, Miss Wong. I felt sorry for her because her English was so limited and on top of that she stuttered. It was impossible to understand the lesson at all. As a result, I lost my confidence in the subject. Prior to joining the school, my maths had been near the top in the class, and as a result I was promoted to the Science and Maths stream, had I stayed on at St Clare's.

Still I did what my father asked and applied to Northcote Teacher Training College. There were written tests involved as well as an interview but I did not remember them being difficult. A couple of weeks later, as I arrived home one afternoon from school, my mother handed me a letter. It was from Northcote Teacher Training College. I was advised that I had passed the tests and had done well. They invited me to join them from September. Without any hesitation, I tore up the letter, threw it in to the bin and told my mother not to say anything about it to my father. I was rather cross that the door to a music school was shut whilst the door to Northcote Teacher Training College, which I had no intention of attending, invited me in!

My secondary school exams were coming up in the summer of 1967. I decided that without any hope of going abroad to study, like my many friends at school, it was important that I do well and I tried to study even harder. Unfortunately, during this crucial exam period, large scale riots broke out in Hong Kong from May to September. It started with some pro-Communist Trade Union workers in the factories wanting more wages and better working conditions. The matter was badly handled by the Hong Kong Government. Chinese Communist Party supporters joined in to support the trade unions against the ruling colonial British.

Every day, there were roadside bombs and petrol bombs planted by pro-CCP demonstrators. A few police officers and several civilians were killed by the bombs and several demonstrators were killed in the raids. As many of the bombs were made in communist-leaning schools, the Governor of Hong

Kong ordered these schools to close. The Cultural Revolution was looming across the border and the country was in turmoil.

Our important exams were not cancelled even though anxious students like me were terrified of the future. Having heard from Nanny about famine and extreme poverty in China, I felt very insecure about everything. We were told to listen to the news if exams were taking place or not. I remember during one exam, there was a group of communist Red Guards shouting outside our School Hall where Exams were taking place. As there was a walkway outside the Hall, we could see these young communists marching across holding red books in their hands and shouting in Putonghua (Mandarin) which we did not understand. It was terribly unsettling and no one, neither my parents nor schoolteachers could give us any answers.

The secondary school exam results were disappointing but not unexpected. It was almost impossible to concentrate as one had no idea if the Exams were on or not the next day. I was very anxious and fearful of what the current turbulent social and political disturbances would lead to. Many School friends were going abroad to study to secure a better future. I was aware that Hong Kong was a British Colony and so we might have to be returned to China tomorrow and sent to work in the fields. This was what the intellectuals and well-off Chinese living under the Communist Regime were subjected to. Almost all my predicted subject grades dropped by one. I was convinced there was zero chance that I would be able to get into the only university in Hong Kong.

Here I should like to mention that the way we learned to pass exams in 1969 was totally by rote. We had no past papers to practise on so we could be better prepared. I still remember how daunting it was when you turned the exam paper over the first time in the Exam Hall. Timing was also a tricky issue as I do not recall any teachers talked about exam technique.

My father had already decided that he would not be able to finance my dream of studying music in the UK. My eldest brother was in the midst of his college education in the US and my father was already struggling to finance his education, so he had to work in the summer to make ends meet. I remember how anxious my mother was when the college fees were due. In fact, she had to sell all her jewellery to pay for his first year's education in the U.S. and there was nothing more she could sell. In the meantime, I had already turned down the Teacher Training College offer which my father had suggested. So the only sensible alternative for me was to remain at the same school to start their Sixth Form. With the vast migration of students abroad, they were more than happy to offer me a place. This would then allow me time to work out what to do with my future.

I did not enjoy the Sixth Form subjects: English, Chinese and History. Having learned by rote throughout the secondary school education, I found thinking for myself almost impossible. What exactly did the teacher want? I tried very hard to put down all the facts I knew without understanding or analysis. This, of course, was not successful and I felt lost — I could see black, white but couldn't understand grey!

Not long after I started the Sixth Form, I learned that the school offered a Commercial Course which would lead to a secretarial career. Apparently, my cousin, Helen, followed this path and had done very well, working as an Executive Secretary of the Managing Director of B.A.T. (British America Tobacco Company). So I decided to have a try.

The course was run by another nun who gave us some lessons on secretarial work, but she was mainly in charge of the admissions. I think her role as the Course Director was to ensure her girls in the class all achieved a reasonable shorthand (100 wpm — words per minute) and typing speed (40 wpm) and then immediately land themselves with a job after graduation.

The only teacher on the course was a shorthand and typing instructor. She was a lovely lady from Burma called Miss Lin. She was always dressed in her national costume. This consisted of a little Chinese jacket, short sleeves in the summer and long sleeves in the winter, with beautiful gemstone buttons. She would match this with a wraparound skirt reaching down to her ankles. Her hair was tied neatly in a bun at the back. She gave me the impression that she was very proud of her country. Prior to meeting her, I did not recall seeing many Burmese people living in Hong Kong at that time. The only Burmese living there were Buddhist monks.

Indeed, in those days there were hardly any non-Chinese people living in Hong Kong, just a few from Pakistan and India, some of whom were Sikhs. In fact, there was a Sikh Temple and an Indian Temple not far from Happy Valley where we lived. Chinese people in Hong Kong were very prejudiced against people from India and Pakistan. They regarded them as "low" class. As I was growing up, the security guards outside banks and residential buildings (including where I lived) were all Indians. The local residents called them "Ah Char" — a rude name denoting their dark skin. My mother, though, was never rude to the Indian security guard of our building. She gave him a little tip now and then even though we were by no means wealthy.

Miss Lin had a soft voice and was very gentle and kind. She was always encouraging and respected each girl's individual progress. Her soft voice, combined with the occasional coughing fits did not make it easy to hear her dictation. Luckily, as I have a relatively good ear and a solid English grammar base, I was able to make good progress. I still remember she told us from the beginning of the course that when we woke up each morning, we must look ourselves in the mirror and tell ourselves "we can achieve a faster speed today, we will do it and we can do it!"

And so, with this motto, my speed in both shorthand and typing went up and up every week and by the end of the year, I had achieved 150 wpm in shorthand. In order to ensure I was secure, I actually passed the Pitman's exam of England twice at 150 wpm. My typing speed, on an old and heavy manual typewriter was 56 wpm. This was equivalent to 120 wpm on an electric typewriter. I ended up being the girl with the fastest speeds on the course.

With such high speeds, I thought I would apply to be a verbatim court reporter. I knew this would be a very secure job with excellent pay. However, being a government job, I had to wait for openings and this could take months. I was anxious to find a job quickly so I could help out with the family's finances. I was rather frustrated that even with such exceptionally high speeds in shorthand and typing, looking for a secretarial job was not as easy as I had thought. I asked the Director of the course who was monitoring every girl's job opportunity after graduation the reasons. She told me that it was because I looked "too" young and laughed. She advised me to be patient and unless asked by the prospective employer, not to attach my photo.

4

STARTING WORK AND LEAVING FOR THE UK

I FOLLOWED the Director's advice and in a couple of months after graduating from the commercial course, I landed my first job as secretary to the Manager of the insurance department of a British firm. They were an insurance arm of the Phoenix Assurance Company in London (which is now part of Sun Alliance). The manager had to share my services with the British representative, also based in Hong Kong. More importantly, I was able to contribute to my family's expenses. I gave half of my monthly earnings (HK$600, UK£60, equivalent £1000 today) to my mother.

The job was interesting, especially dealing with claims after car accidents. I learned never to buy a mini Cooper ever, as accidents in these cars all led to the drivers being killed and the car was a complete write off!

Working with the Australian manager was quite easy as he was always extremely easy-going and took long lunches. He told me that back at home, he would have a swim or do some surfing on the beach at lunch time! He would generally finish work at 5:00 or 5:30 p.m. whilst the rest of the staff at the insurance department were still working away. The British Insurance Representative from London was, on the other hand, quite the opposite. He worked very hard and had lots of correspondence which required churning out many letters. However, because

I was fast, he was very impressed with both my accuracy and efficiency every time he gave me work.

After a year, I felt I had learned what I needed to know about the nature of my job and I looked around. I became a legal secretary in a well-regarded British law firm. The solicitor I worked with was very arrogant. He dealt with commercial clients, mainly Contracts, and the work was not terribly interesting. He knew I was fast and he liked to challenge me with incredibly fast dictations. It was fine but I didn't like his attitude. I thought he was a typical Colonial British who was cold and regarded himself as superior. I decided I had to look for other opportunities as I really did not enjoy the job.

I had a school friend who had left for the UK a year before. She had just finished her secretarial course in London. I was in correspondence with her and I wanted to know if I could also go to London to do an advanced secretarial course since I had already completed my year of secretarial course in Hong Kong.

I chose Pitman's as I had good speed exam results from this renowned Institution and the Courses they offered were relatively inexpensive, compared with my friend's Secretarial College. I wrote to Pitman's and was immediately offered a place by the Principal. The next challenge was, of course, to ask my father to finance this. Mother was always supportive and she did a fabulous job to persuade my father to agree, mainly because it was only for a year. The amount required was £900 (about £15000 today) and a return air-ticket. I think both my parents realised that their daughter had ambition to study abroad and did not give up after the first attempt to go for the Royal College of Music. They believed that this would satisfy my ambition.

Getting onto a chartered flight on Caledonian Airways in 1970 was my first experience of flying. It was very exciting indeed! At last, instead of looking up at the sky staring at the plane which

took my brother off to America and school friends off to Canada, US or Australia to study, I would be up on a plane myself. I was not upset to leave home but I carried with me a big dream as the plane took off from Kai Tak Airport as I waved goodbye to my family and friends.

Kai Tak was famous as Hong Kong's first airport, built in 1925, on the Kowloon side of Hong Kong harbour. It was so close to the city that pilots had to fly in between the tower blocks, so low that passengers could see the televisions inside the apartments, prior to banking sharply just before landing on the short runway. Pilots had special training to be able to land at Kai Tak. It was absolutely amazing that there were no crashes ever!

On arrival, I immediately deposited the cash my father gave me at Barclays Bank. The large amount of cash I was carrying was hidden inside a secret pocket in my undergarment which Mum carefully had sewn on. I

Kai Tak Airport Friends' sent off!

61

was very surprised that they gave me a bank deposit book and the amount I deposited was entered in hand-writing! When I left Hong Kong, HSBC, the largest bank in Hong Kong had already started to computerise and my savings account was printed. In fact, my second eldest brother, Alex, was amongst the first batch of recruits to join their Computer Training Programme.

Later that day, following the visit to Barclays, my school friend in London and her newly married husband took me to a Catholic Hostel within a short walk from Notting Hill Gate Underground Station. This was a convenient place to live as I could travel to Pitman's on the Underground. The hostel was run by Catholic nuns who were not particularly warm or friendly. I recall with a degree of horror that the nun who received me had long whiskers and I wasn't sure if she was a man disguised as a nun! She told me where meals were served and took me to my room which I had to share with a Singaporean girl. She

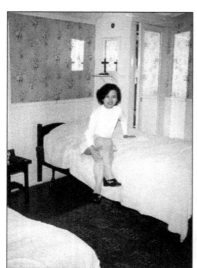

Hostel in Notting Hill Gate. Visit to Hyde Park
London – 1970

was doing a Course at another Secretarial College. The room was rather big but really dark and had heavy wooden furniture. I remember the closet was so huge that several people could easily hide inside. My school friend and her husband left shortly after I had settled in.

I remember the first meal in the hostel was rather simple — a vegetable soup and a stew (with hardly any meat) served with mashed potatoes. My room-mate was very friendly but her English was rather strange, I thought she spoke with a weird sing-song accent. Although she also spoke Cantonese, some of the words she used were totally different from mine. She called bread "Loh Tee" — I believe that must have come from Malaysia as Singapore is a very multi-cultural city. The first night away from home started to hit me. Because Hong Kong was a busy place and my home was always noisy with lots of people around, the sound of silence was really unpleasant. It felt like a piercing sensation into my ears!

The next day I ventured into a nearby shop. I wanted to buy some ice-cream but on return to the hostel, I discovered what I had purchased was a cup of rather sour and unpleasant tasting thick liquid. It turned out to be yoghurt which was something I had never tasted before.

The following day was registration time at Pitman's Central College. I found my way to the college without any difficulty. It was located at 192 Southampton Row. My underground stop was Russell Square and I had to walk across the Square to the College which was rather pleasant. On arrival, I was told to wait outside the office of the Registrar although the letter of acceptance was written by the Principal.

The Registrar was called Mr John Hurst. He was aged around fifty, of medium build, and his face was rather red. He was extremely kind and friendly. After looking at my papers, he looked up and asked me why I wanted to join the College. He said he rarely came across students with such high shorthand and typing speeds.

I was rather anxious and worried that it was all a mistake and that I might be asked to go home. Instead, Mr Hurst asked if I would like to work for him instead as he was looking for a Secretary. The College was very international and the thought of having a Hong Kong girl speaking good English and having such astonishing skills already in shorthand and typing would be an asset to the College.

His offer took me by total surprise! My immediate response was that I only possessed a "student" visa which I was sure would not allow me the right to work. Mr Hurst told me not to worry as he would write me a letter to the Home Office to confirm my employment. He said I should present this letter to them that afternoon and he told me the address where I should present myself.

On arrival at the Home Office after lunch, I presented the letter from Pitman's and my passport to the Officer behind the Counter. I was then told to sit down and wait. It wasn't long before my name was called and I was given the passport back. I looked at it and saw an official stamp on a previously blank page. This was a clear approval that I was allowed to work.

I left the Home Office, went to a nearby phone booth and telephoned my friend. I told her what had been happening since she and her husband dropped me off at the Hostel. She said she could hardly believe my story and I remember she asked me to study the stamp on my passport again. She kept on saying to me "Are you really really sure it is a work permit"? She said that Work Permits were very difficult to obtain and normally took a long time to process. Yes, yes and yes was my reply and that was the start of my very first journey to the UK.

I shared an office with an English girl called Mandy. She worked for the Principal of the College. She was twice my size, had freckles and long hair. She looked reasonably tidy and was friendly towards me. She was a smoker and I noticed that she would light up at tea breaks which happened twice a day.

The College had an international staff. There was a girl from Cape Town called Ruth but everybody called her "Rufus". There was also an Australian girl called Jan. They were all very friendly and chatted a lot about their personal lives which normally involved boyfriends. As I had no interest in boys, I didn't feel I had much to contribute to their conversations. They all smoked except me and they asked me to try it out. I refused as I remember my parents didn't smoke and didn't think it was good for girls to smoke either.

Work for the Registrar was rather interesting at the beginning. It mainly involved writing letters either to accept or reject applicants. The Registrar would hold meetings regularly interviewing candidates. If he thought the candidate was suitable for the course and had a reasonable command of English, it was an acceptance letter that I had to produce.

It wasn't long before I learned how to churn out all the necessary letters on behalf of the Registrar. As months passed, I recall I did nearly a hundred letters a day for him. Tea breaks were, to me, a waste of time. Yes, I did like English tea but it would take me only a few minutes. After I drank my cup of tea, I would return to the Registrar's office and from time to time, I would find him pouring a bottle of rum into a glass. This bottle of rum was in the bottom of the left-hand drawer of his desk. So tea break was rum break! I discovered later that he was previously a Naval Officer!

A year passed by very quickly and I was again feeling anxious about my future. Although I was told I could attend evening shorthand classes free of charge at the College, I found that the speed the class was doing in the evening was much lower than my qualified speed of 150 wpm.

Life in London was rather lonely until my cousin arrived. She wanted to follow in my footsteps into a Secretarial College. So the two of us moved to share a flat in Finsbury Park. It was in an old building and we had a bed-sit in the front of the house. I remember we had to feed the gas meter with coins. On some occasions, when we did not have the right coins, the room was freezing!

I always reflected on my job to see if it was going anywhere. After ten months at Pitman's, I didn't think there was much more to gain. I was literally doing the Registrar's job whilst leaving him to enjoy talking to young girls coming for an interview. So I made the decision to return home. I was paid a salary of £90 a month at Pitman's and I had saved the £900 my father gave me intact. On arriving home, the first thing I did was to give him back all the money with a thank you for the opportunity I had been given. Next, I began to look for new job opportunities in Hong Kong.

Although I did not manage to do an advanced secretarial course at Pitman's I was not at all disappointed at having spent ten months there working instead of studying. It was, in fact, an eye opener and I had also gained a lot of self-confidence.

First of all, I found the English people extremely polite and helpful which was a bit of a surprise, compared with those expatriates I met at work in Hong Kong. Secondly, I did notice there were different English accents within the English class system, i.e. staff and colleagues at Pitman's vs. those who served food in the College Canteen or newspaper sellers in the London streets or shop-keepers. I was quite amused at the beginning to hear people working in the Canteen addressing me as "love" all the time. Thirdly, I discovered that London is very cosmopolitan. In Hong Kong, there were mainly Chinese people and there were also some Indians living there. I had never come across any black people before I came to London. Lastly, I learned that England was an extremely cold and misty place. Living in an old house and having to feed the gas meter was quite expensive, cumbersome and difficult especially if one had a modest income.

5

RETURN TO HONG KONG: WORK AND TRAVEL

I WAS DELIGHTED to return to Hong Kong and, without too much difficulty, I immediately landed a job as Secretary to the Managing Director of another British trading firm. They were agents for building materials, such as "Pilkington" Glass from UK and "Nylex" Formica from Australia. Working for the Managing Director was well-paid (the experience of having worked in London seemed to have made a difference in salary) and that enabled me to make a greater contribution to the family pot. One of my younger brothers was planning to go to college in Canada and we were just about able to afford to finance him. My younger sisters were also beginning to work and so my parents were able to finance two sons studying abroad.

The building material trade was a prosperous one in Hong Kong at the time. Australian and English building materials were highly regarded. As Hong Kong's economy grew, demand for office buildings and residential properties was sky-rocketing. The job of the Managing Director mainly involved submitting tenders for building materials of impending building projects. After a year, I found that my job was, once again. very repetitive. Worst of all, I felt I could no longer tolerate the horrendous swear words (especially when the proposed tender was unsuccessful) used by the Managing Director. I gathered that he apparently had a history from a rough military background. Although his poor use of the English language was not directed at me, it was nonetheless very unpleasant day after day.

The next job I managed to secure was in 1972, as an Executive Secretary to the Managing Director of an American Merchant Bank which was just opening an office in Hong Kong. This was, for me, the "springboard" to my banking career and enabled me to leave a secretarial role at last!

The Managing Director of the merchant bank was from Chile. He was extremely warm, charming, and efficient with his calculations and financial analysis. I understand that he came from an upper-class family. Our first loan was to one of the largest shipping magnates in Hong Kong, Mr C.H. Tung (who later became one of the CEOs of Hong Kong after the colony was returned to China). There were three other expatriates in the Office, one was an Operations Manager from the bank's Head Office in Chicago. He always spoke in a direct but very soft and polite manner. One was an American lawyer, very smart and cultured. He loved Japanese wood block prints and invested in Japanese art objects. The fourth one was a quiet Corporate Finance Manager from London. Everyone worked extremely well together and the office had a fantastic and energetic atmosphere. I felt that was my first truly happy and fulfilling job! I couldn't wait to go to work in the morning and I finished usually after 7:00 p.m.

The days and months flew past like a flash and after a year, I had a closed-door meeting with the Managing Director. It was unusual when he asked me to shut the door behind me. I knew I was doing well but was unsure about the bank's success in getting more business. I was aware how high our overheads were. Other than the four expatriates, we had four other local staff and an office in Central which had a high rent. By the way, the site where our bank was located was actually the same site where my father used to work. My father's old office building of four floors was pulled down and replaced by our new office building. I still remember climbing up some wooden stairs with my mother to visit my father at work!

At the meeting, the Managing Director told me the shocking news that he and the rest of the expatriates were soon to have to return to their offices in London and Chicago respectively. This was because the Bank had been successful in purchasing a local Banking Licence, which had been lying dormant for years. It belonged to a large American insurance company. This meant that the Bank would become a fully-fledged bank, able to take deposits, for example from people in the street. However, it would take a year or so to finalise the legal and administrative work in compliance with the banking regulations in Hong Kong.

My initial response was of total dismay and disappointment. I was so enjoying the job and didn't want to have to leave. However, almost immediately the Managing Director asked if I would be good enough to consider staying on and managing the Bank for a period of up to a year until the Bank officially opened. I was very excited about the offer but I told him I would need to give it some thought. I did not know anything about accounting, for example. We had an accountant, and I was sure that her work had to continue, perhaps in a more simple manner. My boss was not worried about my concern and told me that I could learn it very easily. He would make sure the accountant explained her work carefully to me over the next few weeks before she left. Also I would get full support from the Accountant in their Tokyo Office who would come to visit Hong Kong regularly. In addition, I was able to keep the existing office assistant to support me. What's more, he also promised that I would be able to join the commercial bank in an executive role when it opened.

It was a tricky evening when I got home full of excitement as well as doubts and my parents were not able to offer any advice. In the morning, after my usual morning exercise of running up the hill, I decided to take up the challenge and said yes to the Managing Director who was greatly relieved. I truly felt that there would be opportunities waiting for me when we eventually had a commercial bank which could handle all types of banking transactions.

Over the next few months, I started to learn about our accounting system which was actually not that difficult. Every month end, I had to present statements to Head Office after reconciling our bank's and clients' accounts. The continuance of the Hong Kong Office actually gave confidence to our clients which was important. It also facilitated easy communication with our solicitor over any legal issues on the business front.

I must have done a splendid job as when the transition period was over, I was rewarded with a visit to London and the Bank's Head Office in Chicago!

This was my very first business trip and a very memorable one too. It was particularly pleasing that the commitment I made to the Bank was fully acknowledged by the Managing Director of the London Office.

I was booked into the Cumberland Hotel in Marble Arch, and I remembered I had a rather uncomfortable experience there. It was a very busy business-type hotel and, on one occasion, while I was waiting in the hotel lobby for a colleague to meet me, a stranger came up and wanted to offer me a drink. I was very suspicious of his intentions and I told him I was waiting for a colleague. He quickly realised I was not available to be picked up. I told my boss what had happened. He was alarmed and immediately moved me to a different hotel, small and quiet.

The next day, the American lawyer who worked with me in Hong Kong invited me to his home in Kensington for dinner. He lived in a beautiful house on Victoria Road. I especially remember the very elegant dining room covered with a stunning deep red wallpaper which matched really well with the traditional English walnut furniture in the room. I also tasted, for the first time, a cold soup starter—Vichyssoise, which I thought was rather strange, as Chinese people would never have cold soups. It was considered unhealthy!

Visiting Chicago was most exciting too. The bank was the oldest and largest bank there and had around four thousand employees. Although my visit was not significant, but, unbeknown to me at the time, it paved the way for me to return as one of the bank's trainees several years later.

Whilst I was there, I had a chance to visit my eldest brother. After graduating from his Computer Science degree in Wisconsin, he had joined Sears Roebuck, a very large retail store in Chicago. His office was located on the 72nd floor and to visit his office, one had to change lifts twice! Sears Office was in the tallest building in America at that time and it was the tallest building I had ever visited.

It is worth mentioning that prior to joining the newly opened commercial arm of the merchant bank I worked for in Hong Kong, called UBOL (Underwriters Bank Overseas Limited), I had to visit Sydney, Australia to sort out my migration visa. It was an important trip for me as I had applied to migrate there to follow two of my sisters who had moved there a year before.

Everyone in Hong Kong of my generation was aware that one day, Hong Kong would be returned to China. Those who had a chance to migrate abroad to Canada or Australia, usually took this life-changing step for the sake of their future. It was useful to know that once we lived in Australia for a short period of time, our parents were allowed to join us. As our parents fled China, it would be wise to consider their long-term future should Hong

Kong be returned to China after 1997. It was a dark cloud in the distant sky but was slowly approaching and a decision had to be made.

Sydney was, indeed, a beautiful city. I was particularly impressed with their new Opera House and the splendid Sydney Harbour Bridge. The weather seemed sunny and warm every day. My two younger sisters both took secretarial jobs and were enjoying living there. I was, however, aware of Australia's reputation for racial discrimination and lack of opportunities for women in senior positions.

Although the environment was lovely, I did not, however, feel any warmth or friendliness from the white Australians when I was out travelling in public transport or in the shops. It was definitely more friendly in London! One of my sisters told me that when she was queueing up at the butcher shop one day, the butcher behind the counter refused to serve her and called for the next customer. It was shocking to hear the story! I also learned that there were not many women in senior positions in the commercial world. Most women did secretarial jobs. Very quickly, I made up my mind to tear up my Australian immigration visa which had been issued to me a year earlier. It was a risk staying in Hong Kong in the long term but I had a promising banking career in front of me and it was worth waiting to see where this opportunity would take me.

Underwriters Bank was located in the city centre, not far from where the Merchant Bank was. It comprised the whole of the ground floor and a lower ground floor of this new building. We had a corporate banking area where I was assigned to work. They called this area the "Credit Platform". This was the core team where business was being generated and was therefore the most important department in the bank.

This banking department was headed by an American banker

from Chicago, called Paul. He was extremely friendly, softly spoken, and had a degree from Princeton. Underneath him was a Chinese American, called Anson, also from the Chicago Head Office. He was very relaxed and reminded me more of an Australian than an American! There were two local Chinese banking officers (recruited locally from a competing American bank). The rationale was that these two local Chinese bankers would be able to bring their own customers into the Bank. Other than me, the only female in the Department was an English girl, called Penny. She was the daughter of the Chairman of Cathay Pacific Airlines, another potential business generator!

Initially, I was assigned some high net worth individual accounts, i.e. millionaires who had large deposits. This included a couple of very wealthy Filipinos who were close to President Marcos of the Philippines. Another important client was the owner of the Hong Kong and Macau Ferry. In addition, I was also responsible for banking relationships with various local Chinese banks. As my experience grew, I was assigned to help one of the two Chinese colleagues to handle a few of his corporate clients. These included businessmen in the jewellery business. It is worth noting that Hong Kong's economy was beginning to take off and Chinese love buying jewellery, particularly gold, as gifts when there was a family wedding. Successful jewellers then used their huge profits to invest in properties. I developed a good personal relationship with these jewellers. I was responsible for analysing their accounts every year for review and approval which was very interesting. I learned how they trade, how much stock they held and the amount of loans they secured from the Bank to conduct their business.

In charge of the entire Hong Kong operation was the Managing Director, an American from New York, called Barry. He was apparently a lawyer before he moved his career to banking. He was extremely charming, intelligent and ambitious and we got on really well. Barry was impressed with my ability to communicate well at all levels, especially with clients. He began to involve me whenever he met new clients, which was very important.

As my career began to take a totally different turn, I felt strongly that I needed to improve myself. I looked around to see if there were any suitable evening courses I could take. I found a Business Management Course which offered different modules including accounting, law, economics and finance. I asked Barry if the Bank would help fund this Programme and he immediately agreed. It took a couple of years but I enjoyed the modules, particularly as I felt they were thoroughly worthwhile. I judged that, at last, my career was taking me somewhere and it was correct not to leave Hong Kong for Australia.

Working in a bank in Hong Kong was a well-respected and well-paid job. The greatest benefit was that I was able to purchase a property with my savings and a low interest rate mortgage from the bank. This was a fantastic opportunity as I was the only child in the family who was able to do that. Shortly after acquiring the property, I moved out of my parents' home in Happy Valley and into my new flat in Chi Fu Gardens on the western side of Hong Kong Island. It was a new property development with 28 blocks of high-rise buildings. I acquired a small one-bedroom apartment on the 18th floor which was valued then at HK£240,000 (£24,000, equivalent to £500,000 now)). It had a lovely view of the hillside from the living room and was very quiet. There was also a swimming pool in the complex and each evening, after work, I was able to do ten laps in the pool prior to dinner, after which I would collapse on the sofa in front of the TV until I could hear the tune "God Save the Queen" and a piercing shut-down TV noise. I then stumbled into my bedroom.

I was pleased I was able to have my very own property which was quite rare for single ladies at that time. However, I thought much deeper into this ownership. I believe the main driving force inside me was really to impress my father. As I basically decided to do things "my way", having turned down the offer of a Teacher Training College he suggested, I felt I had to prove myself to him. Having moved up my career path to become a bank's Vice President, I had not had any complimentary comments from him. Whenever we had a chance to meet for meals, he always kept talking about my older brothers, particularly Alex who, after working his way up at HSBC, was now working in a senior position with Mr C. H. Tung's computer company. There was just one occasion that I remembered my mother told me that my father thought I was "too ambitious", and it was almost a warning than a compliment. On hearing this, I decided that it was time I stopped trying to prove myself to my father. After all, it was he who made me drive myself and I should really thank him for my determination to succeed.

Once again, time flew by and four years later, Barry recommended me to Chicago Head Office that I should join the Bank's training Programme. The Bank employed several graduates each year and they had to undergo some training before they started. It was, yet again, a great opportunity and challenge. The Course was very tough and demanding. All the youngsters on this Programme were recent MBA graduates. They were energetic and ambitious. The bank accommodated me in a studio they owned in one of the twin maize-looking high-rise towers in the city centre, facing the Grand Park. Chicago was a beautiful city and I was able to see my brother from time to time. There was a bowl-like concert platform in the park and once we saw an orchestra perform on a Sunday afternoon.

On my return to Hong Kong, important changes were

awaiting. Barry resigned and joined another bank in New York which was a joint venture of 28 small US domestic banks. I was quite anxious as I felt Barry has always been very supportive and was like an anchor for me. My anxiety following Barry's departure from the Bank did not, however, last long. A month or so later, Barry rang me to ask if I would consider becoming the Hong Kong Representative of the Bank where he worked. Their local Representative, an American, was due to retire and Barry would like someone he could totally trust to replace him and he thought of me.

Another fantastic opportunity had opened up for me yet again! I immediately resigned after a duration of eight and a half years, which was not a bad working record. The Representative Office was a posh one overlooking the Hong Kong harbour. I had a Secretary called Charmaine and after all these years, we are still in touch. She has moved to live in Canada and retrained as a physiotherapist, after her divorce.

As the representative of this New York Bank, I was mainly responsible for correspondent banking business in Southeast Asia and sometimes we joined in syndicated loans (these are huge loans in which several banks would take a share to minimise the risk). Banks had credit lines with each other and my task was to ensure that these credit lines were utilised regularly, and best to the full. This position gave me opportunities to travel to many Southeast Asian countries. In fact, I travelled every other month and the job became more international! I also had the chance to see Barry in New York once a year.

In 1982, there was a sharp decline in the Hong Kong property market which usually was cyclical. We had a share of a syndicated loan to a jeweller cum property developer, called Kevin. He was originally from Shanghai and started a jewellery business in Hong Kong. Like other jewellers, he branched out into property

77

as well as a furniture retail business. Kevin was hard-working and terribly charming; so he was able to persuade his bankers to lend him a total of HK$240 million (£24 million) for a commercial building on the waterfront in Wan Chai area.

When the property market began to fall and Kevin found it difficult to pay the interest on time, the Banks were getting nervous. I learned of a saying in banking — when the rain falls, the banks will shut their umbrellas. This was exactly what happened to poor Kevin. There were a lot of negotiations and financial analysis, but in the end, the banks decided to "call the loan", i.e. demand immediate repayment of interest and principal. It was a very trying time as I had to liaise continuously with Barry in New York on what the banks' sentiments were and, as a small participant, we really did not have an option to disagree with the major banks. As I had a very warm relationship with Kevin and he totally understood our bank's position, he did not take a negative view on us. In fact, he quietly decided that he should give his stock of precious jewels in his shop as a part repayment of the loan due to our bank.

It was a very tense moment when I met with Kevin who handed me a box full of rubies, emeralds and diamonds, worth millions. I took the box back to my flat and spoke to Barry immediately in the evening to decide what to do with it. Barry advised me that I should register myself into the Hilton Hotel in the morning and put the box in a safe deposit box in the Hotel. It was a great relief the following day that I was able to deposit this valuable box in the hotel until Barry arrived from New York.

I felt I was reaching the pinnacle of my career as there were hardly any women in my position. I believe there was one other woman but our paths never crossed. It was whilst working in this job that something happened which changed my entire life.

6

MEETING PETER: FAMILY LIFE AND DEVELOPMENTS

ONE DAY, on January 3, 1983, my secretary Charmaine told me that I had a lunch engagement with a Mr Peter Clarke, who was a Representative from a Danish Bank. I asked Charmaine to find out more details of the time and place etc. A few minutes later, she came back to my office to advise me that it would be at 12:45 p.m. at the bar at the top of the Mandarin Hotel. I was a little anxious about meeting a man whom I had never met before in what I thought would be a crowded Bar. So I asked Charmaine to call Mr Clarke's secretary again to find out how I could recognise him. Charmaine came back to tell me that Mr Clarke's secretary suggested I look for the most handsome man there, and then, by the way, he would be wearing a blue tie!

I arrived at the Hotel at 1:00 p.m. which was a few minutes late. I saw an Englishman sitting there by himself and as I walked in, he stood up and greeted me politely. We exchanged business cards, which was the custom in Hong Kong, and I apologised for being a little late as I was held up on a telephone call to Barry.

Mr Clarke was new in Hong Kong and wanted to know about the banking scene. So I did my best to talk about the way banks handled their credit lines and the economy in brief. The meeting was very cordial and before I realised it, it was past 3 p.m. I apologised to Mr Clarke for having to cut short our discussion as I had to go back to work. Several weeks later, I had a call from him from Singapore, asking if we could meet again for lunch.

My view of the British people in Hong Kong was a negative one as those I met or worked with were mostly arrogant and felt superior to the local Chinese. In fact, when I turned the television on and it was a British programme, I quickly changed channel! That was, sadly, the impact of my dislike of the colonial British living in Hong Kong there. However, Mr Clarke was the total opposite of such English people and out of sheer curiosity, I decided to accept his invitation and we started our courtship. At the beginning, I was just curious as I wanted to know if he was really genuine or was he just trying to impress. As events turned out, this was not a prudent way to find out as, not long afterwards, we fell in love.

As both of us were foreign bank representatives, there were occasions where we would be visiting the same bank or going to the same country to see customers. In fact, it is quite amusing that at one point, both our banks were participants in a large syndicated loan to a New Zealand entrepreneur. We had appointments to see the Financial Director of the company and my appointment was earlier. Apparently during the Finance Director's meeting with Peter, he kept talking about me as he was unaware of our relationship!

After nearly two years as an American Bank Representative, I was beginning to establish myself as a senior bank executive in Hong Kong. My name was beginning to get known in the local business community, and soon I was recruited to be a Vice President of another Bank which was owned by a very wealthy and political individual from Jakarta. This organisation was even more ambitious than the Americans. In addition to banking, they invested in properties too. The Bank was run by a very smart Filipino Managing Director, who used to work in a large American Bank. This position meant increased marketing responsibilities in Southeast Asia and mainly on the corporate business side, rather than bank-to-bank business.

It was a challenging role and more business travel was involved. Unfortunately, being an aggressive organisation, there was a lot of politics inside. Competition within the Bank was, in my opinion, excessive and I felt challenged by another American Chinese colleague working side-by-side. He didn't like being a Team member. It was not a particularly pleasant atmosphere in which to work; nonetheless, I battled on and did my best to develop business strategies, reaching out to customers and so on.

Unbeknown to me, the bank had managed to acquire a Bank in San Francisco at the time. With my previous banking representative experience, the Senior Management decided to offer me the position in their newly acquired offices. They thought this would be a good solution to resolve the apparent difficult relationship with this colleague.

On the career front, this was the golden opportunity that I had been waiting for. In fact, it would have been a dream come true for me. I had turned down the opportunity to leave Hong Kong for Australia, for fear of the future when Hong Kong would be returned to China. To move to the US would be brilliant. This decision would, once again, be a life changing moment.

Whilst I was working in the two previous American Banks, I had the pleasure of visiting my friend, Cecilia, from the Hong Kong Law firm we both worked at. She had since then moved to San Francisco and married a local American called Donald. San Francisco was a beautiful city with a lovely warm climate. There were some similarities to Hong Kong in that there were trams running and the city was quite hilly. I really loved the Golden Gate Bridge, which was particularly spectacular during sunset.

My friends also took me to visit the Fishermen's Wharf and I loved their fresh seafood. I was also amazed to taste the Chinese food in their Chinatown, which was very authentic.

In my conversations with Donald, who was obviously very fond of the Chinese and their culture, having married one himself, he was very complimentary about how hard Chinese worked and how it was the Chinese who helped to build the first railways in America, digging through mountains in the heat of the Californian climate. Almost all the laundry shops in San Francisco were created by the Chinese immigrants. I was fascinated by his stories as I did not know about the history of the Chinese migrants in America. Even today, America has not acknowledged that Chinese helped to play an important part in building the country.

I loved San Francisco following several visits there and I had often dreamed about going there to work one day or, best of all, live there permanently. My eldest brother, Frank, lived in Chicago and it wouldn't be too difficult if I wished to visit him. I also found the people in San Francisco particularly warm, friendly, and free-spirited. The bank's offer was **this** dream come true, had it presented itself prior to meeting Peter!

This time, a real life-changing and important decision had to be made. I was at a crossroad! I knew if I chose to accept the job offer in the US, it would have been the end of my relationship with Peter. I could not see him wanting to move to the US with me. To put it bluntly, I could not see him embrace the American culture at all. He was a very reserved and traditionally brought up English gentleman, a Cambridge graduate. His distinguishing quality which attracted me most was his most gentle and kind demeanour. Whenever we walked past a beggar in the street, he always threw a dollar coin to him. Unlike my own father, the thing that really stood out, was Peter's respect for women.

I remember my father would always say to my mother, who, often had very intelligent ideas, be it in investments or solving practical household problems, that because she was "only" a woman, her ideas were worthless! This has always been a source of their conflict in marriage.

After much discussion with Peter, it absolutely proved my thought about our future life together was the correct one. The decision was crystal clear, and we began to set up plans to get married. I turned down the Bank's offer to follow my earlier dream. The notion that I had left London over ten years before, vowing not to return, was out of the window!

When I announced the news of my decision to marry an Englishman to my parents and my grandmother, they were delighted and happy for me. I think they suspected that would be forthcoming. I recall that on one occasion, whilst I was away on a business trip, Peter invited them to his apartment and made them Singapore Noodles for lunch. This was a complicated dish with several processes. First and foremost, you had to go to the wet market to negotiate with the vendor the weight of the prawns you wished to purchase, and he/she would not understand English! Then you had to peel shells off these fresh prawns, not something many westerners could do. You also had to shred the pork thinly as well as slicing shallots and other vegetables.

I know that the meticulous way Peter worked meant it would have taken him many, many hours standing in the kitchen from an early hour in the morning. I thought he did very well making this complicated dish successfully when he told me over a long distance call, and I am sure this attempt had greatly impressed my family. Besides, Peter had, by now, learned to say a few Cantonese words, like "Nei Ho Ma?" which means "how are you?" in a perfect accent. Unlike the French or Italians, Chinese people are always terribly appreciative when a foreigner tries to speak their language. This was proven repeatedly whenever Peter said his greetings to a Chinese person. He or she immediately assumed that he spoke Cantonese fluently and especially when I stood next to him, assuming that I had taught him well, a compliment I gladly accepted. Those were, and still are, the few words he knew how to pronounce perfectly!

The wedding ceremony took place in a modern Methodist Church in Wan Chai and was jointly conducted by a Methodist Minister, Mr Anderson and Father Giovanni Giampietro (who used to be addressed as "Father Johnny" before he adopted a Chinese name), an Italian Catholic priest who had been very close to our family for nearly twenty years. Not only could Father Giampietro speak fluent Cantonese (using colloquial terms only locals could deploy), he also had a deep understanding of the Chinese culture. In addition, he had a very open mind and understood that I could not be married in the Catholic church as Peter had been married before. Nonetheless he accepted my invitation to take part in my wedding in a Methodist Church.

Femina August 1984

Press announcement of our wedding

At the ceremony, he shared a very deep philosophical thought with us about marriage which I still remember well to this day, nearly forty years on, and we passed this same message to our younger son, Henry, when he got married. The idea, expressed in English, was that "the flickering shadow of candles could not be used to sweep the dust off the street". It implied that our deep love for each other would remain firm when we encounter difficulties in our married life together.

I wondered how a priest, who had no experience of marriage, understood about married life and some of the possible difficulties! "Difficulties" are never in one's mind when one is in love about to be married. This, of course, was the meaning of love he was reminding us about. In fact, he experienced an unconditional love from his mother. He told me the story of how, when he was a young boy growing up after the World War II, he played truant away from school. His mother asked him where he had been when he returned home at the end of the day. He told her that he had been playing in abandoned army tanks and with possibly dangerous weapons left behind by the Germans. His mother was horrified and disappointed with his behaviour but said to him "the naughtier you are, the more I love you, and we shall see who wins"! What a wise mother, and no wonder Father Giampietro said that although his mother could not read or write, she was his greatest teacher! His mother died when she reached a hundred years. What a beautiful example of love for us all to remember!

Father Giampietro had a wonderful sense of fun. I recalled the story he told me which was an excellent example of his cheeky personality. Whilst travelling on the train in the subway, a young boy was sitting opposite him with his mother. The boy would not sit still and was beginning to annoy his mother as the train was moving fast and he could fall. She kept asking him to sit still, to no effect. In the end, she said to him quite audibly to Father Giampietro's ears that if the boy did not behave, the "Gweilo" (meaning a foreign devil) sitting opposite would eat him. In a calm voice, Father Giampietro responded, in perfect Cantonese, that he was a local Gweilo and they don't eat children! The mother was mortified...

For our wedding celebration, we held a Chinese style

banquet at the Foreign Bankers' Club which seemed appropriate as we were both bankers. Close family members were invited, my uncles and aunts from my father's side and the same on my mother's side of the family. My nanny also attended as she was like my family too. Sadly, none of Peter's family was able to come from England to share our happiness. Western friends,

Wedding photographs

86

Banquet at Overseas Bankers' Club, Nanny, Dad and Mum congratulating us

office colleagues, both my piano teachers and friends involved in my piano playing days also came to our home for a western style buffet lunch. We had a spectacular ice carving (two feet long and one foot high) with our names "Rebecca and Peter" displayed on the centre of the buffet table. After lunch and speeches, I played Chopin's "Fantasie Impromptu", a piece which Peter loved. It was unusual, I am sure, for anyone to see a bride play the piano on such an occasion; usually an entertainer would be providing music. It was not, however, meant to be just entertainment for the guests, but my love of Chopin's music as a gift for Peter, who would be my lifelong partner.

We spent our honeymoon on Mykonos, an island which Peter had been frequenting for many years himself. It was a memorable holiday as the island did not have many tourists (like it has today). It had many windmills, and the sunset was the most spectacular view in the world. There was a bar near the waterfront, called "Montparnasse" which played classical music

Waterfront at Mykonos. Sunset at Montparnasse Bar

which added a unique atmosphere to the beauty of nature as the day drew to a close. We stayed with a native Greek family in her very small bed and breakfast terrace house. Every morning, you heard the cock crow, which was so unusual, having lived in a noisy city all my life. After breakfast, we would take a small boat to one of the beaches where we would spend the day.

It was worth mentioning that I left my job prior to the wedding as I was keen to start a family soon at the age of 34. It was also time for a little break from my banking career too. Charles was born in Canossa Hospital the following year and was a healthy baby, to my great relief. At birth, he had light brown hair and blue eyes, just like his father's. However, this colour faded by the time he was around ten months old. He now has brown eyes and hair and is six feet tall. Most people of mixed races are good looking, and Charles was no exception. He had a large head, a sign of great intelligence as the doctor who delivered him suggested. His first word was "Bao", which meant bread! Our life in Hong Kong for a year was a blissful one, not only because I had my family around but also, we managed to have my part-time Filipino helper, Lita, work for us on the domestic and child-care front full-time. This gave me a break from waking up in the middle of the night many times to feed him.

I kept a diary of Charles' progress not long after he was brought home from the hospital. Initially it was to keep a record of his feeds, from milk to solids, sleeping, and so on Later on, I also recorded his first smile, his first step, and other signs of development.

The entry on August 27, 1985 reads as follows "Charles woke up at 4 a.m. He made very little noise, played with his toes for a while and went back to sleep. Good boy!"

In 1986, Peter received news from his Bank that he was to transfer back to the London Office. This was a devastating moment for me as it meant a rather permanent good-bye to Hong Kong where I grew up and had built a rather successful career. On the brighter side, however, I wanted Charles to be educated in UK. Some of their schools were world-famous, like Eton for example. Peter registered Charles at Eton, at birth, as soon as he knew the baby was a boy.

It would be eleven years later, at Eton's invitation, that we drove Charles down to visit the school. It was quite a long journey from Cambridge to Windsor, which was where Eton was. It took nearly two hours. Charles was quite a confident boy by then, and he enjoyed his first visit. A few months later we took him there again, this time for a formal academic assessment which included English, Maths, Science and a verbal and non-verbal reasoning test. I remember that someone I knew, when I was working at Girton, called Daniel, who was a science research fellow, had gone to teach Mathematics at Eton. A week later, Daniel rang me as he happened to be one of the invigilators at the admissions tests, to say that Charles had done very well and he believed Charles would be successful in gaining a place. Yes, indeed, Daniel was right!

Since Charles' birth when we registered him at Eton, he now had a younger brother. The Eton fees were among the highest in the country, and we had to consider our finances. We thought, if Charles were able to secure a Music Scholarship, it would be feasible to consider sending him to Eton, but not otherwise. Since Charles was progressing really well in his cello, gaining a distinction in almost every exam he took, I thought it might be a good idea for him to have a go. The Admissions Office arranged for our third visit to meet their Director of Music, Ralph. Charles spent over an hour with him, playing the cello and the piano for him. Ralph also took some time to speak to Charles about his interest, which was the computer. At the end of the meeting,

Ralph came out of his room to tell us that at this stage, he obviously could not guarantee a place but he thought Charles should have a good chance and should apply formally.

After three visits to Eton, I felt it was time to talk to Charles seriously about this possibility as it would be wrong of us to send Charles for a formal Music Scholarship assessment and then turn down the place if he were successful. As a loving mother, I really enjoyed bringing him up. So deep down, I was not keen to send Charles away to a boarding school even though being a music scholar at Eton was a real honour and his father was rather keen.

I asked Charles what he personally thought about this idea. He told me that if I wanted him to go, he would obey. Since Peter liked the idea, I then told him if he didn't enjoy it, he could come home. Charles' immediate reply was no, even if he did not like it, he would not run home! However, he was really happy at his current school, and he knew, if he was amongst the top twenty per cent of the class (which he was), there was an excellent chance that he would be successful in gaining a place at Cambridge. Further, he added that his aim was to go to Cambridge University, like his dad, and that he was not really bothered about going to Eton. It wasn't important to him. I was very impressed by his ability to analyse matters at this young age and, having set himself such a clear objective, I should support him and let him stay at his current school. It turned out that I was right and five years later, he did gain a place at Cambridge, in the same College as his dad!

7

LIFE IN CAMBRIDGE

WE LEFT Hong Kong in 1986 to return to settle in the UK following Peter's new posting. The journey from Hong Kong to the UK was a very long one. Peter decided to visit his Uncle Julius and Aunt Joan in Auckland, New Zealand, first. We stayed there for a couple of weeks, where they had a simple house in the countryside. Coming from a modern living environment with air-conditioning, etc. in Hong Kong, to live in rural New Zealand, was a rather difficult transition for me. Contrary to my own practice, hygiene was unimportant. My sterilised milk bottles for Charles were next to Joan's bucket of leftover food, uncovered, so she could feed her chickens. Some rotten peaches, picked from Julius' garden, were left on the table, which attracted numerous extremely large unwelcome flies. Julius had a couple of very old cars in his garage and was proud to talk to Peter about them for hours. So, I was quite relieved when our visit ended. After leaving New Zealand, we made a quick stop in Los Angeles, as I was keen to take Charles to Disneyland. To my disappointment, at the age of fifteen months, he was not fond of Mickey Mouse at all! Our next stop was London Heathrow, then Cambridge.

We managed to acquire a small three-bedroom house in a new estate, about five miles north of Cambridge, built by a reputable builder, Bovis. The entire living area was about 700 square feet. The house, however, looked very small with the huge furniture

First home in Bar Hill, Cambridge

we brought back from Hong Kong. The advantage of a newly-built house with low ceilings was, of course, that it was quite warm, which was important, having just moved back from Hong Kong which does not have a cold winter. There was a gas fire in the living room which we never needed to use because we had good central heating. There was a little hatch between the dining room and the kitchen which was a unique feature. The house had a small front and back garden which was important with a young family.

We had friendly neighbours, an elderly couple living in a bungalow opposite us, called Stan and Esme. On the right of our house was a family of Pakistani origin, Warsi and Poppy. Warsi was an accountant who travelled to work in London every day and sometimes came home on the same train as Peter. His wife, Poppy, stayed at home to look after her two teenage children. Poppy was friendly and invited us round to her house for tea from time to time. On the left was a retired couple, Cyril and Eileen. They were both very warm, friendly and soft spoken. Cyril used to be an electrician. They had a shiny, clean, light blue "Honda Prelude" which attracted young Charles' attention whenever he looked out of our bedroom windows or was standing outside the house. He would point to the empty drive when Cyril and Eileen were out and ask me where their car was. As a toddler, his interest was already drawn to cars. I never cease to be amazed that he was able to point out the different makes of cars as we drove along the road, while he was still sitting in a baby car seat! Because of his enthusiasm for cars, we often bought him tiny matchbox cars of different makes which would keep him amused for hours.

Reading was a very important part of our daily activity. Peter would always try to come home on time to bath Charles and, before putting him to bed, he would always read to him. Among Charles' favourite books were *How Many Trucks Could a Tow Truck Tow if a Tow Truck Could Tow Tow Trucks* as well as the *The Very Hungry Caterpillar*. Using some wooden poles, Peter built a swing for Charles in the garden and he enjoyed playing outside when the sun was out. I felt the weather in England was very cold and, even though the summer had arrived, I never had to put summer clothes on Charles.

Life without Lita's help and an active toddler was not easy, especially when I was pregnant with a second baby on the way. As Lita agreed to come to the UK to continue her contract with us prior to our departure to the UK, we started her visa process right away so I could have some help when the second baby arrived. It was a fairly straightforward process and I was absolutely thrilled when her visa was approved.

It was blissful to have Lita back with us. She was extremely hard-working, tidy and could cook well too. She loved to look after Charles again as she had formed a nice bond with him as a baby in Hong Kong. She particularly enjoyed working in the garden which was transformed when she started planting in the flower beds. Lita settled in quickly and seemed content with her new life in England.

Having Lita was like having an extra pair of hands when Henry was born. He was a smaller baby than Charles. He was also born early as the Consultant looking after me said he needed to go to America for a conference and asked for my agreement to arrange an earlier caesarean. He assured me that there would be no risk to me or the baby, even though it was three weeks earlier than the due date, something I had no knowledge about.

Perhaps I had placed too much faith in the Consultant's advice, Henry was born smaller than Charles and not feeding well from birth and, after several days, the nurse warned that they might need to feed him through a tube as he was losing weight. Luckily this did not happen as Henry began to gain weight, albeit slowly. When we brought the baby home, it would take him over an hour to finish 4 oz of milk and he would always doze off halfway through. I felt terribly lucky that Lita was here to help. Life with an active toddler and a crying baby at night, which denied me of much sleep, was challenging.

Four months after Henry's birth, Lita went home for a holiday. She had a family in the Philippines, a teenage boy and a girl who were being looked after by her husband. She told me it was her daughter's birthday and she had promised to be with her. I must add that the normal contract with a domestic helper in Hong Kong was that they were allowed two weeks' holiday at home after a year. I thought Lita was treated like a family member, so I did not question it. I gave Lita half a month's pay in advance in case she needed to purchase presents for her family as well as a return ticket. On the day of her departure, I was surprised that she had a lot of luggage with her, almost the entire wardrobe. I raised the question with her and she said the reason was she had bought a lot of presents for her family.

After Lita went home, I invited my mother to visit us. It would be good for her to see our new home in England as well as her new grandson, Henry. I felt happier and more confident with my mother around although it was very tough coping without Lita's household help during the day and inadequate sleep at night. Thinking back to my extremely busy working life in Hong Kong when I usually worked six days-a-week, I found this was much harder work. Nevertheless, I thought this was only temporary and all would be well when Lita returned.

On the day just before Lita was due to return to the UK, I received a registered letter from the Philippines. Inside was the return section of her air ticket and a short letter from Lita saying that she has decided to stay in the Philippines. She was feeling very homesick living in the UK. She did not return the advanced pay in cash I gave her. It was a devastating blow as it was a terrible let down! I planned to have a second baby when she promised to come to help me in England. Now Henry was only four and a half months old and Charles was barely two years. They were quite a handful without any help, to say the least. Peter usually left home at 6:30 a.m. to catch the train to London and would arrive home at 7:15 p.m.

It was the first time I broke into tears, with the letter and her unused ticket in my hand. After getting over the shock, I knew there was nothing I could do. Mother had to return home and I had to learn to cope. When my school friend, Nancy came to visit, I asked how she coped with her two sons, now teenagers, when they were young. She assured me that time flew past very quickly but I knew her husband worked close by and was never away from home for twelve hours.

Looking back, Nancy was right. Time passed quickly and when Charles was about three and Henry was one and a half, they began playing together. This meant I could relax a little and spend time on cooking and cleaning etc.

I liked keeping the house spotlessly clean with two young children and little childcare experience. I would hoover the house and scrub the kitchen floor daily on my knees as Henry started to learn to crawl. I also demanded that any visitors to our house must leave their shoes outside and put on slippers. This was definitely not a British custom and Peter was, at the beginning, not happy with my request to his relatives on their visits, which were rare. This practice was, however, very common in Hong Kong. As time passed, I was interested to see that the British had adopted this habit and Peter's relatives would even bring their own slippers when they came to visit.

Having to look after young boys without my family around brought a constant sense of anxiety. I recalled whenever one of the boys had a cold, I would take him to the local GP straightaway, as that was what my mother would advise and used to do. On one such Surgery visit, the GP gave me a leaflet which read: *How to Deal with Minor Ailments.* He told me that if I were really worried, by all means bring him down, but read the leaflet first as it would be helpful!

When Charles turned three and a half, we decided to send him to a Montessori School. I heard that they had a unique way of developing early childhood education before they start proper school. I was very impressed with the setup of this particular Montessori School in Cambridge following an initial visit. It was run by a sophisticated lady in her thirties who was the daughter of a retired Admiral. She spoke eloquently and did not aim to sell a place to us at all. She explained the principles behind the Montessori way of teaching. She had three teaching staff and I remember all of them particularly well: Mary, Sandra and Lisa. The school had no more than fifteen children who attended in the mornings only. It was an easy decision where Charles should go when the time came.

The school was in an old church hall in Chesterton. It was clean and tidy. Every child coming in had to change into a pair of in-door shoes or slippers before entering. They hung their coats or jackets on a hook designated for their use. They then went into the Hall and were received by the Principal or Lisa or Sandra. The children sat round the room until every child had arrived. It was very orderly.

Montessori had specially designed educational equipment and, to the children, they would be toys, to allow them to explore, create or learn from. Children chose for themselves which equipment they would like that morning. Once they had made their choice, they were given a mat and their toys would be placed inside this mat tidily before they could begin. I remember Charles had a puzzle which taught him a little geography. After building a small landscape, he had to pour some water round the middle area which was called an "island". On another occasion, he had to build an arch bridge with some wooden bricks which fitted perfectly well together, with a keystone piece at the top. I thought this did require some brainwork! Of course, there was music as part of their learning and fun too.

In the first week, Charles was very tearful and refused to let go of my hand when I dropped him off at Montessori. It was the most heart-breaking experience for a mother in the first few days and I held back my own tears. In such moments, I was very grateful that Liza always came to my rescue with her warm and loving approach. She would sit Charles on her knees, hold him tightly in her arms whilst I waited outside until his crying stopped. His crying did not last for more than a few minutes (although it seemed a lifetime to me). It wasn't long before Sandra, or Lisa, were able to reassure him not to cry and soon he was happy to attend Montessori School.

With Charles away in the morning, life was not necessarily easier because Henry was only nineteen months behind. He was an extremely active toddler and never needed an afternoon nap which was very unusual. He seemed to need very little sleep at night either, compared with Charles. When I put him down in his cot at bedtime, I had to put my hand through his bed guard and place it under his face until he fell asleep. Then I carefully removed my hand, sometimes successfully, and other times not! During the day, Henry was always on the go, following what his older brother Charles was doing, and learning from him. When evening came, he would drop off to sleep sitting on his highchair whilst I was still feeding him. He then woke up in a few minutes and was totally revived until his father came home from work at 7:00pm.

Charles had by now learned all the nursery rhymes in the book and was an interesting and talkative child with an enquiring mind. After bringing his father his slippers when the door opened, Charles would sing to Peter with me on the piano all the rhymes he knew. It was natural that Peter's attention was immediately drawn to him as soon as he entered the house. It was interesting to watch how Henry was quick to draw Peter's attention too with a great big smile on his face. He would, with great excitement, walk up the length of Peter's body with his hands held tightly by his dad. It was so joyful to recall the scene of how these two young boys welcomed their father home at the end of his long day in London. As for me, all the hard work in the day cleaning, washing, cooking, and looking after them was entirely worthwhile!

Charles' time at Montessori School had to be cut short by a year following a call from the Admissions of St John's Preparatory School offering him a place to start sooner than expected. We had an initial meeting with the headmaster and a tour of the school. We both liked the Head and the school environment very much although the idea of boarding after age thirteen was not something we had decided on. I particularly liked the children all looking very sharp in their bright red blazers and grey shorts. Boys wore a red cap too which I thought was very smart.

I did not recall Charles had any issues moving to St John's. He seemed to enjoy his time there and he began to learn to read successfully. I still remember his first book was called *John and Jennifer's Yellow Hat.*

I noticed there was a difference mixing with parents at Montessori and those at St. John's Prep School. The former had parents from different backgrounds. There was a lady from Holland and an Indian lady. There was a good atmosphere when we were standing outside waiting for the children to be collected. The parents from St John's were all white middle-class English. As I collected Charles from school every afternoon, I was quite surprised that the mothers standing outside were not particularly interested in my presence. Many of them would chat amongst themselves and one or two would glance at me out of the corner of their eyes but with no intention to make contact.

One day, whilst waiting outside the school for the children to come out, a lady with a heavy Scottish accent smiled at me and we began to engage in a nice conversation. She had four boys, three of whom were going through the school. The oldest was at the Senior House and had already secured a Scholarship to go to Uppingham School which is a boarding school in Rutland. The third son was also on course for a Scholarship at a Boarding School. Her youngest son was Daniel. Charles liked Daniel very much, so I began inviting him home to play regularly.

Marie and I started a warm friendship too. She was a nurse and had had interesting working experience in Dallas. She told me whilst working in the hospital there, she was horrified at the amount of crime there. She had to deal with gun wounds every night which I thought was appalling. However, she said the pay there was far more generous than UK. She mentioned that her husband did contract work in IT with banks in London. Although the contract work was less secure, the pay was excellent and there seemed to be plenty of jobs around which required his expert knowledge and experience in computing. What interested me most was that Marie and her husband had sold their house and lived in rented accommodation in order to pay for their three boys' private education. As I had very little knowledge of the UK education system at that time, I was keen to know why she had to take this big step. She explained that there was a vast difference between the country's comprehensive schools and the private schools. Her second son was at a local comprehensive school, for reasons I didn't fully understand. I think she said something like the school suited him best. She told me that children at State schools were only given books to take home to read twice a week whereas Charles brought a book home each day. It was important that I read with him every day.

Charles got on well at St. John's and built a reputation for himself as being clever, according to Marie. He and Daniel became very good friends. Daniel seemed to provide every bit of news at school to his mother whereas Charles did not say much after school. Charles also began to get invitations to children's birthday parties. Every term, Charles' report was a pleasure to read. He was a good all-rounder and enjoyed playing games at school and was conscientious about doing his homework. His reading and writing were progressing well. He also started learning to play the cello—a quarter size. As we could not find a chair to fit him whilst he was playing this somewhat large instrument for a boy of his size, we eventually found a waste-paper basket made of rattan and turned it upside down with a cushion on the top for him to sit on. It was a perfect solution.

Another boy, Ben, who attended St John's lived in the same village as us and Charles grew to like him too. The boys played in each other's house from time to time. One day, out of the blue, Charles told me that he didn't think he should befriend Ben anymore. I was astonished to hear this and wondered why they fell out. He told me that Ben told him that his mother was German and they did awful things to the English during the War. Wow!! That seemed like a drastic decision, and I thought his national prejudice needed some correction. I told him, with my quick wit, that I did not like the English people whilst I was living in Hong Kong as they behaved in a superior way towards the local Chinese people, as Hong Kong was a British colony. But my view changed when I met his dad. Jokingly, I told Charles not to have such prejudice, as he might, like me, one day grow up and marry a German girl. We both laughed!

Every Monday morning, the children had to do a piece of writing in class about how they spent their weekends. On one occasion, I was embarrassed to read what Charles had written at school: ".. at the weekend, Dad was working in the garden whilst he was playing. He saw him throw some worms over into our neighbour's garden." His teacher asked me, when I collected Charles from school, if his story about his Dad was true. Indeed, I told her that it was, and that it was because I was terrified of worms, even though they were supposed to be good for the garden. I suspect I got that phobia from my mother who was so scared of maggots in the vegetables that when she spotted one, she would immediately throw the whole bunch of vegetables in the bin right away!

Because Charles enjoyed Montessori School so much and we were impressed by the concept of early childhood education there, we decided Henry should follow the same path too. We sent him there at an earlier age than Charles, when he was only two and a half. This was because we felt Henry was ready and would have someone to play with whilst Charles was at school. Although there was a short span of crying when he first started at Montessori, I was much more confident to leave him with Lisa or Sandra.

Unfortunately, after a term, the Head of Montessori advised that she was moving on, and the school was going to be taken over by another lady. I was very sorry to hear this as I thought she was exactly the right Head for the school. I subsequently heard that she was getting married, and I was happy for her.

I met the new lady in charge of Montessori when Term restarted. She was completely different. Her focus was much more on the parents than the children. I noticed that she was wearing a lot of makeup and designer clothes. What's more, I was aware that she didn't show much interest in the children around her. I think she was more focused on marketing, which I believed was the wrong strategy for running a school like this. But I decided to give her a chance to see how Henry felt. The following week, when I collected Henry at the end of the morning, he looked a little sad but was not able to tell me much. One of the mothers told me she saw Henry cry at the Nursery before I arrived. This confirmed my suspicion that the school atmosphere had changed under the new management. I was very worried about the situation and wondered what I should do next.

One afternoon, I received a phone call from Sandra who was an older and more experienced teacher than Lisa. She advised me that she and Lisa had decided to start their own Nursery School in Fen Ditton, which was a small village very close to our home. Apparently, like me, they were not impressed with the new

Head. They confirmed that they would follow the Montessori style of developing children. However, as they did not have a lot of capital, they would not have the full set of Montessori equipment to begin with, but they hoped they would be able to acquire more later. They wondered if I would consider sending Henry to their new nursery, but he would be their first and only child temporarily until other children joined. I was absolutely overjoyed to hear this and confirmed with zero hesitation. I knew that Henry was already familiar with these two warm and helpful teachers and he would, in time, be the most senior boy there, showing the way to other new children which would be good for him. This was exactly what happened, and Henry was very happy at the nursery for a year.

Henry joined St. John's two academic years after Charles. Mr Mould, the then current Headmaster, retired and a young Head, Mr Jones succeeded him. The school was doing well, and I found all their teachers dedicated and totally excellent. Henry was making good progress academically. He was also exceptionally talented in sport and had a fiercely competitive spirit. This was evident in the annual Sports Day, when he would end up with many different coloured badges on his white shirt having won many different events on the sports field. He was also very popular amongst his peers.

When Charles was six and was in his last year of his pre-prep school, we were wondering about the next stage of schooling. The idea of staying on until he was thirteen at St. John's was questionable as they were preparing their boys to join boarding schools. This was mainly due to the astronomically high fees of boarding schools, unless Charles gained a Scholarship. At that time, private school fees had already escalated sharply. With two boys at St John's, we already felt the severe financial strain.

We were attracted to the high academic reputation of a boys

only day school, The Perse Prep School from which boys could proceed to their Senior School at age eleven. We decided to make an initial visit. We were warmly received by a very tall and serious looking Headmaster, Mr Paul Izzett. He showed us round the school which was in a Victorian style house, previously occupied by the Managing Director of Robert Sayle Department Store. The whole school had around 250 children from seven to eleven years old. It had a lovely learning atmosphere. I remember asking Mr Izzett just one question: how do we prepare our son for the entrance test? His answer was simple and straightforward: we look for boys with a reading age of two years above his chronological age. In other words, he should be now reading books for an eight-year-old.

As Charles always enjoyed reading, we did not think it was too challenging, but we needed just to ensure that the books he was reading were of the right age group. So, we were careful to check the books he would bring home from the Library and confirm with his teacher at St. John's that his reading ability was good.

So, at the age of just over six, we brought Charles to The Perse for an assessment. We had to leave him at the school gate with this severe looking Headmaster standing in front to greet all the boys. I felt more terrified than Charles! He was then led into the Victorian style main building. We were told to leave and collect him at lunch time. He would be given some written papers to do, an interview and the chance to play a game of football. That was the morning's agenda.

When I collected Charles at lunch time, he seemed happy about his performance. He said some children cried but he didn't. He told me one little test he was asked to do, on arrival at the classroom, was to mark a "X" on a map of the building where exactly he was sitting. I thought that was quite a challenging task for a young child, who would find just the arrival experience itself quite daunting. Having to leave the parents at the front of the school and be led by people he never met before into a building he had never been. I was not surprised some children would be in tears. Anyway, a couple of weeks later, a very positive letter arrived from The Perse confirming that he was offered a place to start the next September, which was very pleasing news!

In order to help with the educational expenses, I immediately looked around for a local job. Not long after I arrived in the UK, I remember receiving a call from a head-hunter, wondering if I was interested to work in banking in London. My immediate response was no. I had decided that I wanted very much to bring up the boys myself and therefore the long commute to London from Cambridge would not suit, looking at Peter's time away from home of at least twelve hours every day.

8

A New Career in Cambridge

When I became a mother after I got married, I had three goals in mind of how to bring up my children. First and foremost, to educate them well at a good school and hopefully they would be able to go to one of the top UK universities. Secondly, to give them a musical education, for example, playing a musical instrument or two. I firmly believed that learning to play a musical instrument would help their brains to develop well and train them with a good sense of discipline, as they would need to put in regular practice to be successful. Thirdly, I would like to help them develop "faith" and become a member of the Catholic Church. I knew this would be the hardest of all my three goals to achieve but I wanted to give this a chance. So we, as a family, always went to Sunday Mass. We would normally sit at the last row of the Church. I would bring some colouring pens, drawing papers and books, so the boys did not disturb anyone during the service. Usually, at the end of Mass, people sitting in front of us were very surprised when they turned around and saw the two young boys sitting behind as they were very quiet and well-behaved.

Looking for a job was quite challenging as I was not looking to re-start my banking career where I had a lot of experience. After several unsuccessful applications, eventually an opportunity arrived. Girton College's Bursar was looking for a Personal

Assistant.

Cambridge University is the home of one of the world's top Universities and has thirty-one Colleges. It would be fascinating to work in one as it would allow me to gain an insight into what life was like there. More importantly, how to prepare our young sons so they would have a chance to be educated at Cambridge, like Peter.

I was called for an interview and got on very well with the Bursar, Charles Larkum. He had not long been in the College and had a financial background. He told me he had worked at the World Bank in New York for a few years and he read English at Oxford. He said he had over 120 applicants and he thought we would work together well. He told me that I was the first Chinese ever employed to work in College. So I started working for him shortly after the interview.

Girton College was located on the north side of Cambridge which was not far from home. In order to work full-time, I needed to hire a nanny, at least part-time, to collect the boys from St John's Prep School and look after them until I arrived home from work.

Domestic help is expensive in the UK and we had to pay tax on top of the wages. I felt Hong Kong had a far better system as you could import helpers from other Southeast Asian countries, like the Philippines, Thailand or Indonesia. These domestic helpers were usually untrained but if they were keen and hard-working, it usually did not take long to train or familiarise them with what you wanted them to do. Most of them would do "all" the housework, including dog-walking, as well as looking after young children. Some of them were hired to look after elderly parents too and it was a far better system than placing them in a Care Home.

In Hong Kong today, you pay an overseas domestic helper

the equivalent of £450 a month and a return air-ticket home once every two years. You have, however, to provide them with suitable accommodation and all meals. They have a day off every week, and they all work nearly twelve hours a day! I believe there are Laws and a Tribunal in place now so these domestic helpers are not exploited by the employer. This is the reason why Hong Kong can prosper successfully in their economy as a large proportion of women return to work after they have a family. Elderly parents are also well cared for and they do not have to rely on social welfare which is utilised only by the poorer sections of society.

Girton College was founded in 1869, initially as a women's college. Although women studied there after its foundation, they were not awarded degrees until 1948. The College went mixed in 1979. As the location of the College was about three miles from the City Centre and other Cambridge Colleges, it wasn't a particular popular choice for candidates. However, the College had a residential site called Wolfson Court, next to St John's Prep School, nearer the town centre for their second-year students and some of their Research students, which seemed very sensible. Because it was initially a women's college, the College's financial position was fairly weak. Most graduate women did not have strong money-earning careers. The College relied on some legacies and they were mainly left by unmarried women after they passed away.

With an impressive background in investment and banking, the Bursar was hired to try to improve the College's financial position. The first thing I learned working with Charles was that making changes in a Cambridge College was an extremely difficult, although not an impossible task. On the domestic front, for example, whenever Charles wanted to re-arrange things, usually to save money, the replies from the Housekeeper or the

Maintenance Manager were always, "but Bursar, we have always done it like this…." " To which Charles would explode with anger and there would be long arguments! After many encounters like this, Charles' relationship with the domestic staff started to deteriorate. No one liked him. I was very sympathetic and was very sensitive to his moods too!

An obvious way to improve College income was to raise students' room rents. As the Fellowship of the College was mainly made up of women who were particularly caring over their students, the idea of increasing students' financial burden didn't go down well at Council either! It was clear that politics was at play and Charles was not a popular Bursar, compared to the previous female Bursar who was highly favoured and had been there for many years until she retired, even though she left a legacy of a College about to face financial ruin!

My job for the Bursar was initially mainly secretarial. As time went on, Charles dedicated more and more administrative responsibilities to me, like working with the Music Fellow, Martin, in choosing Choral Scholars every year. There were over two hundred applicants every year. In addition to being academically brilliant, these candidates would need to meet the exceedingly high choral quality requirements and have demonstrated a strong commitment to very disciplined regular choir practices if successful. Many Choral Scholars were able to enjoy the brilliant singing in College's weekly Choral Evensong as well some Choir tours abroad, all paid for by the College. Acceptance as a Choral Scholar was totally subject to the normal academic requirements under the College's regular stringent assessment process. In other words, this was no short-cut in getting into Cambridge.

Girton College was built in beautiful red brick in Victorian architectural style and working there was like going back in time!

There were long corridors on three floors and it was easy to get completely lost. I got to know a bedmaker called Dorothy who cleaned the Mistress' Office every morning. She told me she had been working in Girton all her life. She said in the past, she used to bring coal in the morning to light up a fire for the Mistress to heat up her room. Then she would bring her hot water for her to wash. Often, I would see Dorothy working on her knees polishing the wooden floors. What a contrast to the modern living in Hong Kong where I was brought up!

In addition to providing Choral Awards administrative assistance to Martin, Charles also assigned me to help with the College's Research Fellowship Competition. The College offered two Fellowships each year, one in the humanities and one in sciences. On the humanities side, there were usually close to two hundred candidates and about a hundred in sciences. I had to invite them to send in samples of their research work for the Fellowship's selection. It was very arduous. It was interesting to notice that the science candidates usually came from abroad, either China, Eastern Europe or Russia. The renumeration was extremely modest but accommodation was provided. Clearly one had to be very passionate about the subject to aim for, what I thought, very modest financial reward. On the other hand, this was the role to get into an academic career and ultimately leading to a position in the University as a Lecturer or a Professor.

As well as working for the Bursar, I also helped the Assistant Bursar who dealt with students' finances. This mainly involved writing letters to students who either had problems paying their fees for accommodation on time or requiring a short-term student loan. It was interesting work. My job at Girton was rather full and was certainly different from the banking career I had before. The only challenges I had was when one of our boys was ill and I had to ask for time off. I felt torn whenever it happened as I knew

Charles would be displeased without help that day.

I worked at Girton College for a total of three and a half years, and I was pleased to be in a full-time job for the first time in the UK. Whilst the pay was modest, especially after paying for a nanny, it did enable me to gain work experience and learn about life inside a Cambridge College.

The journey to work in the morning was fairly quick and efficient when I first started but, not long after, traffic in Cambridge began to increase and the driving became quite stressful, having first to drop off the two boys at school.

Girton College was surrounded by very well-tended beautiful grounds. There was an orchard and a pond at the back of the garden. The Receptionist always greeted me warmly when I dropped into the post room near her office every morning. There were two porters on duty in the Lodge and I usually found them polite and helpful.

Like every old institution, there was always politics to contend with and I quickly learned to be cautious and not tread on people's toes. The two departments which seemed to have some dominant power were the Tutorial and the Admissions Offices. They reported to Fellows in charge of students' academic and social welfare in the case of the Tutorial Office and to the Admissions Tutor in the cases of admitting undergraduates. The ladies working there had been there for many years and knew their roles well, including maintaining their traditional convention of long morning and afternoon tea breaks which no one dared disturb. Their doors were shut! It was clear that they would be sceptical of any new changes that Charles, the new Bursar wanted to introduce. For example, the introduction of a new computer system for the Tutorial Office was a real battle!

Whilst working at Girton, it is worth remembering two young Singaporean undergraduates I befriended. One was a girl reading Classics. She knew some Kung Fu which she had learned from her father. I found her demonstration of Kung Fu excellent to watch as my own mother was taught Kung Fu when she was young too. Once she came to our house and taught our son Charles some Kung Fu which was lovely to see. Before she left Cambridge, she gave me the Chinese steel sword she used for her Kung Fu which was a very memorable souvenir. One day she introduced me to her boyfriend, her Classics Tutor, a very intelligent Classics Scholar from Liverpool, who went on to become a university Professor. Unfortunately, this relationship was rejected by her father and I understood they parted in great sadness.

Another Singaporean was a mathematician who was admitted to the College on a Scholarship by the government of Singapore. Apparently, by accepting the Scholarship, he would need to return to serve in the government for three years after graduation. This was in addition to the one-year National Service he had to do as a Singaporean citizen. On his graduation day, he introduced me to his mother who came to share her son's success. She was accommodated in College and one afternoon, I bumped into her and she told me that her son was out, busy socialising with his friends before leaving Cambridge. She had not seen much of him since she arrived in the UK a few days before. I felt very sorry for her and invited her back to our home for a meal. It was very interesting to learn about her background. She said she was a factory worker back in Singapore. Her son showed great talent in maths already when he was still very young. Whenever she took him out shopping in the market with her, before the vendor could work out the sums, her son would already say aloud the exact amount of change her mother should be given back and he was absolutely correct every time!

She told me she was a single mother, bringing up two sons.

She told the factory Manager she wanted some time off work as she was travelling to England to attend her son's graduation at Cambridge University. The Manager looked at her with disbelief and kept asking her to check if she had got the name of the university right—"Cambridge University? Are you absolutely sure?" I saw sadness in her face when she told me that her son had changed and felt quite distant now. She noticed that when he met her at the Airport. Clearly three years' experience living in Cambridge and mixing with young people who grew up in the west had changed him.

I also had the pleasure of meeting the successful Science Research Fellow from Hong Kong. He and his accompanying wife lived at Wolfson Court, next door to St John's Prep School. Lo was his name, and he was doing a PhD in Applied Physics/Materials, focusing on super-conductivity research. It was interesting talking to him about his frustration at times that his research work, which was purely his own, had to have his Supervisor's name on it too. He was not getting as many chances to present his papers as he deserved. From the Linkedin App, I was pleased to learn that he is now a Vice-President working in Silicon Valley, responsible for technology innovation and marketing.

It was also worth remembering a Romanian student, Sabin, whom I met whilst working in College. Sabin flew over to the UK to go through the usual admissions process including an interview, and was subsequently offered a place to study architecture. When the College advised him of this good news, he replied, sadly, that he would not be able to join without a full Scholarship from the University or the College. Instead of the College offering his place to another candidate, many of whom I suspect were equally deserving, the College decided to provide the fees necessary for him to attend the Course and the cost of the accommodation. I suspect that Sabin was rather exceptional, bearing in mind that he would not have had the type of education or resources in Romania to support his ambition to study at Cambridge. I wasn't aware of the full details of the arrangement, but I was sure Charles played a role to facilitate this. Today I am pleased still to be in touch with Sabin, who is working here in Cambridge. In fact, he started his own practice and had married an English wife. He has two lovely children.

On the job front, I noticed that the Bursar's relationship with the Fellowship was not working out well. Charles' normal warm smiles had dwindled over a fairly short time. He was often deep in his own thoughts. He seemed to shut himself in the office often typing away behind his computer for hours and hours while I took care of his routine administrative papers and got on with the work I could handle on my own.

I suspect his plan to revive the College's finances did not receive much support and in fact, had upset many Fellows who were, understandably, all very much on the side of the students. It wasn't easy to raise funds from the alumni either as Girton was set up as a women's College. Not many women were able to land well-paid jobs and, after their marriage, they would often spend their income on the needs of their own families. Although men were admitted in the late 1970's, not many were in careers which would allow them to earn adequate income to enable them to make any significant donations to their College. The extra income which came into the College relied mainly on some spinsters' legacies. For some reason, perhaps because they were unmarried, these spinsters seemed to live a long and untroubled life so the College had to wait for a long while! I see from public records that today Girton's financial position has revived completely as a result of the success of the establishment of their Development Office as well as their investments, the decisions on which were perhaps legacies of Charles.

I saw Charles' turmoil over his job was so unbearable that he started slamming the office door, cursed at the computer often when things went wrong and occasionally leapt downstairs so fast as if there was a fire behind him! The Assistant Bursar and I were getting seriously concerned about the stress he was under. We both thought one day, he would fall down the stairs and kill himself. I remember the only time when he was his normal charming self was after a short holiday. So I always tried to encourage him to go away more often as it would help improve his health, physical and mental. More important, his mood!

Charles' fine mood usually did not last long after he was back from his holiday and I noticed his relationship in College amongst the Fellowship had deteriorated even further as time passed. This was evident in the regular College Council meetings, usually after he had spent many hours preparing the Council papers. One afternoon, as I walked past the Stanley Library, which had a glass door so you could see what was going on inside, I saw that Charles was sitting on one side of the long table alone whilst all the other Council members were sitting opposite him. I felt very sympathetic at this scene and thought this could not go on too much longer.

Indeed, shortly after this, Charles tendered his resignation, but I was delighted that he was immediately offered a position at another College, Sidney Sussex, as their Bursar. After Charles' quick departure, the Assistant Bursar and I took on the day-to-day running of the office. The College appointed an engineering Fellow, Howard, who would drop in from time to time to sign any necessary papers I prepared for him. He was extremely pleasant and had great confidence in us keeping things going whilst a new Bursar was being appointed. In fact, he was so pleased with the results of what I did that he asked me to write my own references for him to sign when I resigned a few months later. That is not such an easy task!

With Charles' departure, I had time to reflect on my own position. I looked at my skills in administration, marketing experience whilst working in banking in Hong Kong, my languages and my understanding of the Chinese and English culture etc. I thought there must be something more I could do to have a fulfilling life here as well as helping the family's educational needs for the boys which was my highest priority.

After finishing at St. John's Prep School, it was time for our son, Charles to move to The Perse. From the time we put his name down at private schools, first at St John's and then The Perse Prep, we noticed the school fees had gone up by leaps and bounds, roughly ten per cent a year over the previous five years. I also found the cost of the childcare and the difficulties of replacing nannies, when they left, was not making my full-time job at Girton worthwhile. I could hardly contribute much of my income to school fees involved.

I decided it was time to find a solution. I was beginning to see more and more Chinese students when I had the chance to go to Cambridge City Centre. I thought coming to study in a Boarding School without any parents around, the schools must require a guardian to care for them. Also, they would need somewhere to stay during the one-week half-term break.

With this idea in mind, I thought I should venture out to establish my own business. This would give me the chance to increase my income towards the educational needs of the boys but also spend the time I needed to look after them in the way I wanted. After Charles started at The Perse, it was time to consider Henry's school too. The decision was quite straightforward, he should follow his brother to an academic day school. I gave notice to St John's and his Form Teacher was rather disappointed. Henry was doing very well there and was so good at sports that clearly they did not want to lose him. Jokingly the teacher commented that we wanted to have Henry beat The Perse in our games! She said she would speak to the Head and enquired if the School could offer him a Sports Scholarship. The idea was tempting but I knew my heart was set at letting the two boys remain in the same school. More importantly, I was reluctant to consider Henry moving on to a Boarding School as almost all of their children would. This was just as well, as the Headmaster told the teacher that the School was unable to offer Henry a Sports Scholarship.

It was interesting to remember Charles' view of St. John's after he had settled at The Perse. To my surprise, he told me he felt much happier at The Perse than St. John's. Reading his termly reports was always a pleasure — he was doing very well in every subject. Henry, too, had made the transition from St John's to The Perse with ease. It was much easier, too, for me to just drive them to only one school. When waiting outside the school gate, I also found the parents at The Perse much more friendly than St John's. They were all ordinary women, like me, making sacrifices so that their children were able to have a good education. I began making friends in Cambridge.

9

CAMBRIDGE GUARDIANS

I NOW HAD to focus on increasing the family income to pay for two boys' school fees. I started visiting UK boarding schools in and around Cambridge to offer my guardianship services under the name Cambridge Guardians Limited. For the sake of the anonymity and confidentiality, I would prefer not to mention the names of the schools I worked with nor the full names of the students whom I would like to talk about. Nonetheless, their stories are worth recording and are all true.

I handed in my resignation notice which Howard and other colleagues were disappointed to read. I was very touched to receive a leaving card from the Assistant Bursar pleading for me to stay. We had been in a rather close working relationship and supported each other, coping with the Bursar's serious mood swings due to his own unsatisfactory working relationship with the Fellowship. Before I left, I remember I met a Fellow in the corridor, who knew I was leaving, and asked me how long I had been there. I told him three and a half years and he seemed very surprised as he felt I had been there for much longer than that. It was heart-warming to know that someone did notice my contribution to the College and was sad I had decided to leave.

I was anxious but at the same time excited about the idea of starting my own business, with Peter's total support. In addition to the financial needs of the family, I felt that the job at Girton was rather repetitive, and it was time to take on new challenges again. However, I knew this would not be easy, as a foreigner living in England. The business venture I decided to start did not require capital and there was, therefore, no risk involved.

I started researching into the boarding schools in and around Cambridge. I also drafted and printed a leaflet to explain my background, my understanding of the Chinese and English culture, speaking three Chinese dialects, my understanding of the education system in Hong Kong etc. I began writing to the boarding schools' Heads and Registrars to request meetings to offer my services. I didn't get an overwhelming response from the schools immediately but a few positive responses which were an encouraging start. I remember visiting the Head of a school in Northampton, who was extremely warm and charming. The School was predominantly a day school for boys but wanted to have some boarders which would obviously help with the school's finances. Boarding fees were usually three times those of day schools. Another relatively small boarding school for girls I visited was in Norfolk.

In my initial discussions with the various schools, I learned that not only was there a need for someone like me to look after some of their Boarders but they also would like to increase their overseas intake. The overseas students, especially from Hong Kong, were all excellent students. They worked hard, had ambitious parents and, because they had a good English language background, most of them fitted in well and contributed to the school's culture. Many of the students were also very talented musically and often played an instrument or sang in their school choir; hence this was another important incentive for the boarding schools to start admitting more Hong Kong students.

The mission of Cambridge Guardians was quite clear right from the start. Firstly, I should aim to offer a supreme guardianship to overseas students, caring for them like my own children. Secondly, the aim was to help overseas students to identify the right schools in England. From my school visits and tours around the school premises, I learned that some schools place an important emphasis on sport, others on music and some have students with strong academic abilities, many of whom would be aiming to go to Cambridge or Oxford Universities (Oxbridge).

Knowing how much ambition Chinese parents have for their children, I understood that many of them would like to send their children to a highly academic school, regardless of the abilities of their children. Entrance, however, would be difficult. The advantage Hong Kong students had was that they were strong in Maths and some of the sciences, but their English comprehension would be slightly weaker, being their second language. Hence it was important that this was explained clearly to the parents so that their hopes could be managed.

To succeed in recruiting students overseas it was important for me to make regular visits to Hong Kong to meet the parents of students I was looking after, and report back to them on how their children were progressing. Cambridge Guardians, therefore, offered me a bridge back to Hong Kong which was wonderful. This would mean I could see my relatives and friends, although by then, my parents had moved away to reside in Sydney.

I remember the uncanny feeling on my first visit back to Hong Kong after so many years. I was very excited but at the same time rather anxious. Hong Kong is a fast-changing city and I still remember when I came back from my business travels abroad after a short space of time, there would always be a few changes. For example, a shop near our home disappeared and a new one appeared in its place. Building work in progress was finished and another site was under construction. This is what makes Hong Kong such an exciting place to live. Almost nothing stood still, except the warmth and love at home.

As soon as I arrived, I re-visited the block of flats where I grew up in Happy Valley, looking out onto the horse racing course. I looked up to the 8th floor where I used to live. I saw the balcony, but no plants were hanging out. The doctor's surgery was still on the third floor. The Buddhist Parlour on the fourth floor where monks and worshippers had regular prayer services was still there. The front entrance had a secured door for which you needed a code to enter the building. The image of the Sikh security guard whom we addressed as "Ah Singh" flashed back to my mind. He couldn't speak any Cantonese but as soon as he saw me or my parents, he would always get up from his desk, press the lift button for us and open the door when the lift reached the ground floor. Sadly, I suspect Ah Singh would have passed away now. May his God keep him in peace.

The shops I used to know had all disappeared except the chemist at the corner opposite our block of flats. I thought about the dry-cleaning shop owned by a friendly gentleman from Shanghai. He was always helpful and reliable. If there were any urgent items where we needed the clothing back, he would always deliver. Up the hill was a bakery, also owned by a gentleman from Shanghai. I used to love his braided sweet rolls with dried mixed fruit and his butterfly puffs too were so delicious! There used to be a famous restaurant across the street which was known particularly for their egg tarts. They were hot and crispy and came out of the oven at 4:00 p.m. every day. People would be queueing outside before they were ready and would buy a dozen, put neatly into a cardboard box. They also sold barbecue pork and duck. The shop had a few tables where construction workers would come for their lunch, which was simply steamed rice with their barbecue meat, served with a delicious gravy, for two Hong Kong dollars. Often one would see a line of very expensive motor cars parked outside this shop, buying their egg tarts or their barbecue meat. Whenever we had unexpected guests for dinner, my mother would ask me or one of my siblings to go across the road to buy this as an extra dish for our guests. In place of all the interesting shops near us, as described above, there were now lots of estate agents' offices, clearly making enormous profits from the expensive properties in this highly desirable residential area.

I walked up Sing Woo Road which was just round the corner from my old block of flats, towards the market where my mother and I used to do our daily shopping. I used to go with her at weekends or on school holidays to help her carry the food back. The shop which used to sell beef had disappeared. I still remember that the man with grey hair who owned the shop knew exactly what my mother wanted as soon as we arrived. He always gave us a warm greeting and would give us the best cuts of beef. They were all hanging up on large hooks on a rail at his eye level. He would wrap the beef my mother asked for in paper and tie it up with a piece of straw. The next stop was to see the woman who owned the vegetable store further up the road. Although there were other vegetable stores nearer, we would never use them as my mother did not feel their owners were honest. My mother would normally buy some "Choy Sum", a bunch of fresh green Chinese vegetables suitable to serve with a quick stir-fry of the sliced beef with oyster sauce, a delicious dish we all loved. The woman weighed the bunch of vegetables on a scale which consisted of a plate where you placed them, with the appropriate weight moved along to the other end of the long stick until the vegetables on the plate balanced with the correct weight.

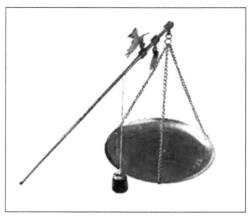

Weighing scales – 1960

Today, the little side street where all the various market vendors used to trade had completely disappeared and in its place was a concrete building up the road marked "Happy Valley Market". I could only look at the building with a big sigh but kept the sweet memories of the market and its vendors stored carefully in my mind!

It was interesting to note that in 1995, when we started, I was almost certainly the only professional Chinese-speaking Guardian in the UK. In the past, parents sent their children to Schools in the UK and then looked for someone, often a friend who lived in England, to be their son or daughter's Guardian, to satisfy the school's policy. The child would be able to live in their friend's home during the half-term holidays but their friend would not take a serious interest in the child's education. After all, it might create a rather difficult relationship with their friends. They would, for example, not attend any parent-teachers' meetings.

Not long after Cambridge Guardians was established, we were invited to join AEGIS, the Association for the Education and Guardianship of International Students. Peter became the organisation's financial Secretary. The object of AEGIS was to set up professional standards and guidelines so that the child was protected and the school, too, would feel more confident that he or she would be properly looked after. As a member of AEGIS, my reputation as a caring and responsible guardian began to spread. The number of children under our guardianship grew steadily year after year. In the 23 years' history of Cambridge Guardians, the numbers grew from one or two students to forty-two. These students attended different schools in and around Cambridge. They came from mainland China, Hong Kong, the Middle-East, Russia, Taiwan, Malaysia, Indonesia and Singapore.

Whilst the business in Cambridge Guardians was developing well, I was very surprised when I received a phone call from Charles, the Bursar I used to serve at Girton. He was now happily settled at his new position at Sidney Sussex College. He asked if I would work for him as their new Conference Manager. He understood I had a marketing background in banking and most of all, I think he had complete trust in my ability and loyalty to him. Conference business at Cambridge Colleges was a new phenomenon but an ideal way of increasing College's income. After all, when students left for the Easter and Summer Holidays, their bedrooms were left empty. In the meantime, College had to continue to pay College staff.

I advised Charles that I needed to think about his exciting proposition but as I had started my own business, I needed to think how this would work. The care of my own two young boys was always my top priority. What about the school runs and, in addition, I had no help at home. Peter was working full-time in London. Bursar Charles re-assured me that he would be quite flexible. The solution I offered him was that I would only work part-time, from 9:00 a.m. to 1:00 p.m. He seemed happy with my idea and I started right away.

Once again, I was the only Chinese staff ever employed by Sidney. Unlike Girton, not all the staff at Sidney Sussex were friendly. Obviously, they were aware that I had previous connections with the new Bursar, so they had to be careful not to disclose too much information to me which they suspected I might pass back to the new boss.

Sidney Sussex was located right in the city centre. I was allocated a precious car park space which was crucial, bearing in mind how expensive or tricky it was to park in the City Centre. It was also necessary for me to arrive at work on time, after first dropping the boys at their school in the morning. Unlike Girton, it did not have large grounds but the College had a beautiful garden with colourful flowers planted in their flower beds. They had several gardeners who did a superb job which meant the colours of the flower beds changed according to the season. It was such a pleasure to walk through the garden after I parked my car each morning in the College car park located right behind their garden. The College also had a beautiful old courtyard which fitted well with its four hundred years of history. The students had to walk a mile to the sports field which the College shared with another College. There was no swimming pool, either, unlike Girton. The College front wall was adorned by the beautiful Wisteria when they started to blossom each year! It was a convenient and beautiful place to work. At the end of a successful conference season, I was often awarded a modest bonus. I did, on one occasion, jokingly tell Charles that I might need to pay him working here!

It was good to work with Charles again. This time, he was a changed person. He was much, much happier at Sidney Sussex. The College was also in a rather poor financial state because the previous Bursar, who had been there for many years prior to his retirement, had not raised students' rent for years. So my job as their first Conference Manager was to help to provide the badly needed income! This was a challenge, but I was confident as I had the full support of Charles.

Following Oxford University's successful business strategy, Cambridge also set up a Central Conference Booking Centre. Anyone needing to find a venue to hold a conference sent their requirements to the Cambridge Conference Centre who would, in turn, email all the Conference Managers and it would be up to them to bid for the business directly.

Although Sidney Sussex was in the city centre where many conference guests would prefer to be located, we would not be able to offer many en-suite bedrooms; so large organisations that required hotel-like accommodation with a Cambridge College atmosphere, were out of reach for us. This was our greatest disadvantage. I discussed this with Charles and he advised me that College already had plans to address this. In the meantime, I would only be able to bid for conferences which had a lower budget but liked our location. I decided that I also had to offer a competitive rate, due to competition from other Colleges. The conferences which I was successful in getting were mainly of an academic or educational nature. The key thing I learned from this type of conference is that they often are "repeat" business, which was an important business stream. Every year, I would look at the inflation rate and kept the conference rate at an attractive level so they would return the next year. Another very important aspect of the conference trade was to get to know the organisers and their needs. It was also vital to communicate the specific needs of each conference to the staff working in the College Kitchen, the Buttery (where wines were arranged) and the housekeeping staff.

I also learned how important it was to balance the College Fellows' needs as some of them would want to hold a short

Sidney Sussex College Staff Photo – I am fourth on the left

conference too in their own College during the holidays, but they would not wish to pay anything, if it could be avoided. This was always a struggle!

Although I only worked four hours every morning, I felt I put in a whole day's work in the College. All other Colleges had full-time staff dealing with conference business. However, I was equally ambitious and did not want to let Charles down. Many responses from the organisations I contacted which were interested to book a venue often commented that I was the very first Conference Manager to contact them. This gave them a good impression of my efficiency and confidence to use us.

In a relatively short time, I was beginning to fill up all the bedrooms during the vacation period. The Catering staff, Porters and the Housekeeper and her staff had to work much harder to serve the conference guests. In some respects, I became rather unpopular by increasing staff's workload. Rumour was going around that I spent the morning chatting away on the telephone and then I was off for the afternoon. Indeed, that was my job to speak to potential customers to persuade them to come. I also faced some antagonism from the Head Porter running the Front Lodge. I did not feel they should treat our customers like they did the students. A typical greeting to a student of "what d'you want" must not be applied to a conference guest. This arrogant attitude towards our paying commercial customers would not do! I brought this matter up with Charles and he was very understanding and said he would find a way to deal with it. Once again, he had learned that making changes in a four hundred-year-old College was difficult.

I remember on one occasion, as I was in the Porters' Lodge collecting my post, the Head Porter deliberately put his foot out as I walked past to trip me up. No apology was given either. Fortunately, I managed to maintain my balance, but it was quite apparent that he had ill feelings towards me.

The hostility of the porters gradually changed. Apparently, Bursars from other Colleges were also facing similar difficulties with the build-up of the Conference trade. So, the University arranged a professional training course for Porters. This was finally happening, and I was pleased that things were going to improve.

Although the College Kitchen had to work very hard, having to serve hundreds of meals as soon as Term ended, their attitude towards me was completely different. I believe the main reason was that I understood the intense pressure they were working under and let them know at least two weeks in advance of the upcoming events so they could organise deliveries and extra serving staff. I was also very quick in telling them if numbers changed and all the relevant details they needed to know. Instead of being tripped over when I was at the Porters Lodge, I was greeted with big smiles when I walked in and was often offered food, be it my favourite fresh pineapple on a stick from Nick or being asked to taste a new recipe the Head Chef had just prepared.

It was very satisfying to see the success of the conference business even though we were constrained by the limited number of guests rooms. It didn't bother me what other College staff thought about my part-time job there.

One morning, I was walking along the cloisters of the College and met a Chinese gentleman in his sixties, called William. I greeted him and we started to chat. He was the very wealthy entrepreneur from Hong Kong who owned the franchise of National Panasonic. He and his wife came at the invitation of the College Master to attend a special Foundation Dinner. The Master was setting up an exclusive club, called the 1596 Club with the aim of attracting donations from wealthy individuals.

William was thrilled to be able to speak Cantonese with me. He said he was fed up with the English food that he had been served in the last couple of days and asked me where he could get some authentic Chinese food. I told him that none of the Chinese restaurants in Cambridge would meet the high standards of the Chinese food he had in Hong Kong. I invited him to dine at our home if he would like. Without hesitation, he asked to come and bring his wife and please would I not tell the Master!

Instead of me cooking for William, he asked if he could cook me an Indian meal. He asked me to purchase various ingredient he needed, and he spent several hours making curry in our relatively humble kitchen.

I also got to know his wife, Serena who was a highly intelligent lady and we shared the same love of classical music. Serena was trained as a Soprano, singing arias and her academic subject of interest was Freud. We developed a very close friendship and after the couple left for Hong Kong, Serena would ring me and we would speak for hours on the telephone about her family. Her relationship with her husband had deteriorated and was close to breaking point.

William gave the College one and a half million pounds sterling and the College built a Conference Hall in his name. This was wonderful as it would give us an impressive meeting room to add to our other modest conference facilities.

My life became exceedingly busy — working in the College in the morning, collecting the boys after school, preparing family meals, cleaning, washing and ironing. I remember once Charles reported that his friends at school were always complimenting him on his shiny shoes. Indeed, I was very proud that all the gentlemen in the household had shiny shoes, even though it was near mid-night by the end of my working day — it had to be done!

On top of looking after the family, I also worked hard on developing the guardianship services. Amongst the first students I looked after was a boy from Hong Kong, aged thirteen, called Edward. This family was introduced by the Head of a school near Northampton. It was predominantly a day school but they wanted a few boarders. Northampton was about an hour's drive away and I thought it would be manageable. The visits to the school were normally at weekends when Peter was home to look after the boys.

Edward was a lovely and polite boy. His parents did not speak much English and, like all Chinese parents, had big ambitions for their son. It was the normal culture in many Chinese families that children's education and upbringing remain the mother's responsibility whilst the father would be totally concerned with bringing in the necessary income. Mothers would always report to fathers the progress of their children. With Edward studying in the UK, and his younger teenage sister at school, their mother, Linda, used to spend her spare time playing mah-jong with her friends. She was quite superstitious and would not wish to speak to me on the phone about school, as it might bring her bad luck, and lose money to her friends at mah-jong. She would always call me back after the game was over.

Edward's father had a garment manufacturing business which he jointly owned with his brothers. The factory was located in China and their garments were sold locally. So, having a Cantonese speaking guardian was a lifeline for Linda. She told me that initially she would prefer to send Edward to a top Boarding School, rather than a predominantly day school which was lower in the League Tables. Unfortunately, Edward's English wasn't good enough and he was introduced to another school which was looking for just a few boarders.

In the early days of Cambridge Guardians, I also played host to a few students during the school holidays. I had one spare room in the house. This gave me the experience of providing for the students' needs and the opportunity to develop a very close relationship with them and their parents.

One of the students I took care of in the holidays came from a Boarding School in Cambridge. Unlike Edward, his English was excellent and he was quiet and extremely hard-working. His name was Steven.

Steven's parents had no education. They owned a shop which sold BBQ pork and duck, like the famous one in Happy Valley. Their shop was located near construction sites in Kowloon Peninsula. They had a few tables inside the shop which would allow workers to come and have their meals. This set-up was just like the famous barbecue shop near our home.

Steven's parents' business began to flourish in a housing boom. From a small shop selling quick lunch meals for workers, with high turnover, they turned themselves into a fully-fledged restaurant. As they were situated in a newly developed area, there were many construction workers around. They opened another restaurant elsewhere targeting lower income customers but probably with high margins. With the income they generated from the restaurant business, they began investing in properties which was immensely profitable at that time in Hong Kong. The property business was a cyclical one but provided you had enough money to pay the mortgage when the market went down so didn't have to sell, the market would almost always rise to reach a new high.

With increased population growth in Hong Kong, there was a huge demand for the government to provide for more housing. Land in Hong Kong was controlled by the ruling British. They rationed the sale of land and there was a small cartel of several property developers who would bid for the land once it was released. They met privately to determine the price they should bid prior to the land release which I doubt was legal in the West.

Some wealthy investors often could make up to twenty per cent profit over the price of the property even before the building was finished, if they were able or quick enough to put down a deposit to buy at the planning stage. I remembered seeing queues from early morning outside property development offices, when new apartments were being offered for sale. These investors would put their names down and paid the five per cent or so deposit, then wait. Often investors would sell their newly acquired properties to new buyers once the building was ready to move in and take the profit. This was the quickest and easiest way to become rich in Hong Kong. Almost all businesses had an interest in properties of one sort or another. There were no technical skills required but just enough money to put down the first deposit and you could repeat the same over and over again. However, the difficulty was to have saved enough for the deposit for the investment, which was not easy. The banks in Hong Kong were all super conservative and would not lend to their customers without collateral or for speculation purposes. So the property business started to be the privilege of only a precious few.

Steven was the younger of two sons in the family. When he was born, his parents were working flat out in their restaurants and shops, often more than twelve hours a day. Their elder son was looked after by a lady who lived in a poor Council flat. So Steven, as a baby, was brought into the shop whilst his parents worked. His cradle was placed on the top of the shop's rice barrel. As Baby Steven grew bigger, one day he fell into the rice barrel! The lady who was looking after his older brother saw what happened and took pity on him. She told his parents that she would like to take him home and look after him as well. The parents were greatly relieved and enormously grateful. Steven lived with this lovely lady and was taken to see his hardworking parents in the restaurant in the evenings, seven days a week. He built a strong bond with this lady as a result and I noticed that he would call her from England regularly.

Unlike his brother, Steven was academically bright and was doing very well at school. Although his parents had hardly any education themselves, they were keen for Steven to be able to develop his full academic potential. From a modest local primary school, they were keen to send Steven to a better school so that he would be good enough to study abroad one day. They knew the reputation of an excellent international school in Hong Kong and they arranged for him to apply. As they did not speak or write any English, I was certain they would have asked their friends to help them fill in the application form and follow the necessary admission procedure etc.

Steven clearly did very well in the written test at this renowned international school. The next stage was an interview with the Headmaster, who was not Chinese. Steven was able to respond well to his various questions. The very last question was an odd one. On Steven's application form was the address of the lady who looked after him and it was a Council flat address in a poor area. The Headmaster asked Steve if he was aware of the fees his school charged!

As I grew up in a large family, it was quite normal to have many children around. During school holidays, I had to cook more food at meal times and do more washing etc. Charles and Henry seemed to get on well with Edward and Steven. The four boys all enjoyed football and often would play together well in the field behind our back garden.

On one occasion, I had to accommodate a boy from China over half-term. As China had a one child policy then, I had heard that their children were often spoiled. I knew of this challenge as their Guardian. The name of this boy was also called Henry. He had good English and had a gregarious nature. He spoke with confidence and was keen to learn, which was great. However, it was clear that he did not understand English manners. He would go into Charles' or Henry's room, often without knocking. This made Charles, in particular, uncomfortable, especially with student Henry's loud speaking tone. Charles complained to me as he was beginning to feel annoyed that he was regularly disturbed. I said I would talk to student Henry. I said to Charles, however, that he had to learn to be more tolerant of other people. Imagine if he were to go to a boarding school, he would have to deal with many such "Henry's" annoying behaviour whereas he only had to put up with student Henry during the one week of half-term. I thought this was good for Charles to learn too.

Edward's English was improving in leaps and bounds through interaction with our sons. It was very funny to record that one day, Edward wanted to share our son Henry's bag of crisps after a game of football. Unfortunately, he was unable to pronounce crisps clearly. Instead he would say "could I have some crips" to which Henry refused. He said he would give some to him only when he could pronounce "crisp" clearly. That evening, I gathered Edward practised and practised in his room and the following day, he asked Henry again could he share his crisps to which Henry said "Yes!" Our Henry was, of course, quite a few years younger and smaller than Edward.

One day, Linda rang me to say that I needed to go to the school immediately to speak to them as Edward was being bullied by a Greek boy and this was not the first time. Apparently, Edward and this Greek boy were not seeing eye to eye and the relationship had come to a breaking point. One evening, the Greek boy poured some cold water over Edward's face whilst he was asleep. I was furious to hear this and immediately called his Housemaster to discuss this incident and to find out what was going on between the two boys. The Housemaster was excellent. He investigated the incident immediately and arranged to meet me. The Greek boy apologised, and I was pleased that prior to leaving the school, Edward and the Greek boy became good friends.

After spending three years at the predominantly day school in Northampton, Edward's English and academic progress had greatly improved. He was particularly talented in Maths and his ambitious mother, Linda, asked for my help to find a better boarding school for her son. This wasn't too difficult as after GCSE it would be normal to change and go to a different school for Sixth Form. In fact, it would often be easier to get into a good school then rather than at age thirteen.

Edward changed to one of UK's top boarding schools. He excelled in all the chosen subjects and had the potential to fulfil his parents' ambition to apply to Cambridge. Like many Chinese parents, they would like their children to study either Medicine or Law. I discussed Edward's passion for his subject and it was absolutely clear to me that he should read Mathematics. He had no interest whatsoever in Biology or Chemistry. He told me that he was terribly scared at the sight of blood and the horrible thought of being sued if he made a wrong diagnosis of his patients.

It was very difficult to convince Edward's father and make him understand his son's decision to apply for the subject he loved, i.e. Mathematics. His father was absolutely furious that Edward refused to change his mind. His view was that if Edward was predicted four A-level subjects at 'A' grades, surely he was good enough to read Medicine (whether he liked it or not!). He was not convinced that I was right to support his son's decision to study Mathematics. I understood his relationship with Edward was turning very difficult when he went home for the summer holidays.

At school, Edward started to develop an interest in a female student in his class who was good looking and bright and was aiming for Cambridge, like him. When Edward came to live with us during school holidays, I noticed that he was more aware of his appearance. He asked if I considered him to be good looking and how he could improve. For example, should be change his hair style etc. He told me that he was very disappointed that the girl he was keen on at school would not meet up with him when they were back home in Hong Kong for the school holidays. This girl told him that her mother was very ambitious for her and she needed to work hard, even in the holidays. Her mother told her that dating with boys should be left until much later. At school, however, this girl would meet up with Edward for coffee and the two had an enjoyable time together. I warned Edward that he should not put his heart and soul into this girl but focus on his upcoming interview at Cambridge instead. It was clear to me that the girl was only treating him like her toy, to be played with at her leisure. I could see this fell on deaf ears when a teenager experienced his first love.

On the day of the Cambridge interview, I brought Edward to the city centre on my way to work at Sidney Sussex. I suggested he study in the Library whilst I worked in the morning. To my surprise, he asked me where he should go to get a souvenir for his girlfriend! I was furious. I warned him again that his girlfriend would gain a place at Cambridge, and he wouldn't if he did not focus on his interview.

When Edward came out of his Cambridge interview, he told me he should have done better. He was asked three questions. He knew the first one. He felt had he revised, he would be able to answer the second question as he remembered he came across it before. Because he stumbled over the second question, he was beginning to panic and he told the interviewer that he was very sorry that he couldn't answer the third question. I was pleased to learn that Edward was put in the Cambridge Admissions Pool (for a second chance if another candidate didn't achieve the grades although the chance was very low) which indicated to me that he had the potential to be admitted had he been more focused. When the Cambridge results came out, Edward told me his girlfriend had been successful which wasn't surprising. It was a hard lesson for poor Edward, but I was happy for him as he was admitted to Imperial College, London, onto the four-year course which led him to a Master's Degree. I gathered he did extremely well and was now a top financial professional in Hong Kong. It was sad though that his father refused to talk to him for more than a year!

Steven also consulted me about his choice of subject at university. He told me his school was advising him to apply to Oxford to do a Geography course. Steven was interested to become a town planner. Growing up in the industrial area of Hong Kong and living in a much poorer area, he was keen to make improvements. Upon research, he advised me that he wanted to apply to Cardiff University, instead of Oxford, as it had a fantastic Town Planning Course. His mother called me on the telephone and told me that she would totally agree with me if I thought Cardiff University was the suitable choice for her son. I told her she had a fantastic son and whatever the outcome, he would do very well. Today Steven is a senior town planner in the Hong Kong Government, and I was so proud to be invited to his wedding and sat at the top table with his parents.

A very interesting relationship, which I had developed in the early days of my guardianship service with a boy and his parents from China, was a memorable one. His name was Charles, the same as our elder son. A mother from China, for whose son I was Guardian at the time at an excellent public school, contacted me and asked if I would be good enough to help her friend's son to find him a good school. She said this boy was just twelve years old and I agreed. She introduced me to meet Charles. I was impressed that he spoke good English and was confident. He told me he came from Shanghai.

So with some basic personal information, I contacted the Head of a small prep school in a Suffolk village who was keen to have a few more boarders. I had met him some time before when our son, Henry, played a football match there once representing his school. I was very impressed with the Head, following conversations with him, after the match was finished. He kindly invited parents from the opposing school to his reception room to have tea. The school was housed in a lovely Victorian style building and had beautiful grounds. They even had an outdoor swimming pool which was quite rare. It had just under two hundred pupils, many of them day students. I thought for a young child whose English was not his first language, it would be an ideal place to start, as classes were quite small and there were lots of opportunities to learn the language and the culture. What's more, I really liked the Head who was very warm. I compared him with our son's prep school head who, although revered, was at the same time, a little fearsome.

After my introduction Charles was, without any hesitation, accepted into the prep school and started in September of the same year. A month or so later, I was very surprised to receive a telephone call from the Head one morning. He asked me, in an intriguing manner, how much I knew about Charles' background. I replied that all I knew about him was already relayed to him when I introduced Charles to his school.

He told me he had just spoken to the Registrar of one of the top public schools in the Rutland area. He told me Charles was registered there and had already been accepted for a place the following September. Unfortunately, his place at this distinguished school had suddenly been withdrawn! What's more, he told me that Charles had been living in the Newmarket area, very close to his school, at a horse-trainer and his wife's home for a while. At that moment, the penny dropped! I recalled Charles knew where Suffolk was when I first met him and told him that there was a prep school in Suffolk that I would contact on his behalf. It did strike me, at the time, that he knew where Suffolk was when I asked him about the geography of England. Most of the students for whom I was guardian usually had no idea of, for example, where their school was located. All they knew about England was London.

I thought what the Head told me was very mysterious and decided to visit the school right away. More importantly, I must speak to Charles immediately as well as his parents directly. On arrival at the school in the afternoon, the Head gave me a private room where I could speak to Charles.

Charles explained to me candidly this time that he had been

living in England for several months before meeting me. Indeed, he was staying in Newmarket with the horse-trainer and his wife who became his English teacher. This couple went to China and had recruited a couple of students whom they brought to the UK. The students stayed with the couple and learned English at their kitchen table every morning. The aim was that they would learn English with the family, who would arrange to find them a good school. Whilst Charles was living with the couple, he and the other older boy from Beijing played tricks on the family, whom they disliked intensely, and so they behaved very badly.

Charles said his teacher was rather mean to him and the other boy. For example, if he didn't want to eat the egg at breakfast and gave it to his friend to have instead, he would be told off severely. To get back at their English teacher, one day the boys quietly slipped orange juice into cups of coffee and tea when the family was having a party and there were guests present. Charles also admitted stealing some money from the horse-trainer at the suggestion of the older boy. They took £60 which was lying around the house. Charles kept twenty pounds, and the older boy had the rest which he used to buy a pair of trainers.

This latest incident of theft was the last straw for Charles. The next day, his teacher rang the Registrar of the school which had offered him a place and told him how badly behaved Charles was. She particularly emphasised that Charles was not remorseful and would be a bad egg at his school. As a result of this information, the school withdrew the place for Charles. This was a devastating blow to him. When Charles returned home in the holidays, he was severely punished by his father including a slap on his face. He said it was the very first time his father had become so angry with him.

The conversation with Charles' father was very revealing. He told me that he was a senior official responsible for developing the new airport in one of China's largest cities. As China had a one child policy at the time, Charles was his only child, a boy, who was the family's most valuable asset. He told me that his wife also worked for the government.

Charles was sent to a local School. His parents' dream was to have their son educated in the West and learn more English. I would imagine Charles' parents would have gone through the cultural revolution and suffered in unimaginable ways, like many intellectual people at the time. I was sure "freedom" would be very much in their minds. As civil servants, none of them would be allowed passports out of China. So they had to rely on agents to realise the dream for their son.

Another fascinating bit of information from Charles' father was that because of his important position, his son was often showered with gifts from many people who wanted favours from him in his project. Teachers at school were also careful not to be critical of his son. As such, it was impossible for him to discipline his son the way he wanted to as no one ever reported to him that his son could be naughty. He knew, because of his background, it would not be easy for Charles to develop well. He was already seeing him being badly spoilt by so many gifts. As such, with his friend's personal contacts, he decided to let Charles go to the UK, aged eleven, with this couple from Newmarket who was introduced to them. He told me that he was exceedingly pleased that his friend had introduced me to him as he had heard about my professional reputation and more importantly, my ability to communicate with him in Mandarin, his own language. This was the start of a long and successful relationship between us.

The next step I took was to contact the school which had withdrawn the place for Charles to certify the situation. I spoke to the Registrar who already knew me. He said he did receive information about Charles' bad behaviour in his English teacher's home. What made him withdraw the place was that he was told that Charles was not at all remorseful for his theft and other bad behaviour and that he would be a terrible influence at his school. He told me that Charles even wrote a letter to the Headmaster threatening some form of revenge when he grew up. This letter expressed his shock at his father's anger with him which he had never witnessed previously. It was, in his opinion, all due to the school withdrawing the place offered to him. The letter stressed that the Head should immediately re-instate the place to him or when he grew up, he would … The letter ended up with a "Merry Christmas" to the Head! I asked the Registrar to send me a copy of this letter which he did. When I saw Charles at school, I asked if he wrote the letter himself, as I felt that the English was surprisingly good for a twelve-year-old from China. He confirmed he did and, for words he didn't know, he looked them up in the dictionary.

It was clear to me that Charles was a very bright boy and would have a great future if he was educated properly and walked down the right path. I told him after our meeting that I would help him to find an equally good school but with one important condition. I wanted him to start behaving well every day. Like a scout, he should do at least one good deed each day. I would like him to record his kind deed in a diary which I would come and inspect. If I learned that he was becoming a better boy, I would definitely get him into an excellent school. If he continued to be naughty, I would send him back to China when he completed his prep school. I also emphasised that if he worked hard, with his intelligence, he would, one day, become a leader of his country. Conversely, he would end up behind bars! Which would he choose? I gave him examples of how he could be kind and helpful to the teachers, boys and girls at the school.

Charles turned out to be a success at the prep school. His

English improved rapidly and he was also good in all his subjects. With the strong recommendation of the head and with good Common Entrance results, he was offered a place at an equally top English public school near Peterborough.

Although it was clear to me that Charles had turned around in terms of his behaviour, life in a boarding school for a teenager from a foreign country was not straightforward. He was sometimes caught in fights with other boys. He told me the main reason was that sometimes boys made racist remarks against him. Once, he felt he had had enough of such attitudes from other boys, when a boy used foul language against him and his mother. He lashed out and punched the other boy in the face.

It was good to see how his Housemaster handled the incident. Charles' attacker apologised to him and he also spoke to other boys in the House about respect for other people's culture. The Housemaster was also aware that Charles had short fuse and was very sensitive. He organised for Charles to be on an anger management course at school. During the time I was looking after Charles, I communicated with his father in China regularly on the telephone and by e-mail. Charles spoke to his father daily. His father wrote him a little book containing steps of how he should handle himself when in difficulties.

On the academic side, Charles was improving in leaps and bounds. I was very proud that my predictions for Charles were correct and that he would have a bright future with a good education and a supportive family. In a short period of time, Charles was awarded an English prize which was a great achievement for a boy for whom English is the second language. He began to be respected around the House and was given responsibility from the Housemaster. He was an officer in the school's Combined Cadet Force. He was growing from strength to strength. After Charles finished his A Levels, in which he performed exceedingly well, he gained a place to read bio-chemistry at Oxford, realising the dream of his wonderful and supportive parents.

Whilst at Oxford, Charles taught Polish immigrants English in his spare time. Upon his graduation, he got a job in the City of London in the finance sector. His parents had retired and moved to England to live in a large house with him in the countryside. Charles' parents said they would never forget how I had helped their precious son when he was under water and that his success today was largely due to my genuine love and compassion towards him.

I never thought being a Guardian would require a detective mind, but I did find that on one occasion, I would need to start being a detective.

As with many of the students under my guardianship, James came through parents' contacts. He was from Guangdong province, southern China. His mother worked in the Meat Export Bureau. All of Hong Kong's meat came from abroad; but almost all their pork was imported from China. Pig farmers had to comply with certain export standards and the permission to export their pork was very much reliant on the important "stamp" from James' mother in the Export Bureau. I was almost certain that there would be a small amount of corruption and brown envelopes stuffed with cash changed hands for certain farmers who might not quite meet 100% of the standard. This was quite common thirty years ago throughout China. Today, the situation is almost certainly different as corruption is dealt with very seriously and is no longer widespread.

I managed to get James into a reasonably good boarding school in Essex, but it was subject to his attending a language school for three months prior to attending, to ensure his English was good enough to cope with the GCSE curriculum. I was very pleased that I managed to enrol him in a language school which I knew well in Cambridge.

When I met James on his arrival, I was a little surprised. He certainly did not look thirteen, as his mother advised. He was tall and looked quite mature. Furthermore, he looked as if he required to shave bits of hair which was appearing round his mouth! After settling him in his host family and giving him some time to get over his jetlag, I asked to see his passport and to my surprise, it stated he was thirteen. However, I was not convinced that was correct looking at James. So, I picked up the telephone and called his mother. She told me that James was actually fifteen years old. Before sending him to the UK, she had heard from her friends that because of the different education systems in China and the UK, students from China were one year older than their counterpart in the UK, and she thought this might preclude him from getting into an English school.

To my knowledge, there was, indeed, normally a one-year difference in age between Chinese students and English students at the equivalent academic level, but most schools in the UK would not have a problem. Today, schools in England would not accept students who would be close to eighteen when they joined the Sixth Form. This is the age when they legally become adults and would be allowed alcohol and could engage in sexual activities.

To facilitate James' journey to successfully join a school in the UK, James' mother felt she had to forge James' age on his Birth Certificate before applying to the Passport Issuing Authorities. She said if James were a year younger than his biological age, that particular year was deemed "inauspicious", so it had to be the year after. So, James had to be two years younger on his birth certificate and passport. I suspect this would require some exchange of brown envelopes containing cash with the official issuing the birth certificate for James. I reported my findings to the school who accepted him for September entry, but they didn't seem to be concerned. They advised me that they would rely on the information on his passport.

James seemed to enjoy attending the language school I found him. The atmosphere there was relaxing; the teachers were well-experienced in teaching foreign students and he was able to meet students from other countries.

One day, I received a call from the office of the language school advising me that one of their female students had reported to them that James had borrowed a large sum of money from her and had refused to return it. The girl was very distressed and upset as she was unable to pay her living expenses.

I thought this was a very serious matter if it were true. I called James who immediately denied the allegation. I then wondered if this girl was trying to obtain money from James, having formed a close relationship with him. According to the language school, they did befriend each other. In order to find out the truth, I asked the language school the name of this girl in question and the address of the family she was staying with so I could do some investigation myself since James had denied it. One afternoon, I went to visit the family where she stayed, unannounced, as I didn't want her to know that I was coming to question her. I thought there was a better chance to find the truth if I just appeared suddenly to question her.

A man opened the door after I explained myself and let me into the house. He was the host for this girl. He told me the girl was upstairs but before I went up to her room, I had a little chat with him. He was pleased to know that I was James' Guardian and was hoping that I would sort this out. I asked if he knew James. He said he did see James come to his house three times but he did not go to the girl's room. The girl went upstairs to her room when James arrived and went out with him. He was very sad and sympathetic with the girl who was struggling to pay him her living cost. She told him that James was her boyfriend and he needed to borrow some money from her. Because James denied having borrowed the money from her, she now had to work at MacDonald's so that she could earn some money to pay the landlord.

After speaking to the landlord, I went upstairs and knocked on the girl's door. I told her who I was and she let me in. Almost immediately, she burst into tears and told me her side of the story which was exactly what I had learned from the Landlord downstairs. She and James had been dating for a couple of months before he left the language school to join the mainstream school. James had asked her to lend him some money. He told her he needed to pay his guardianship fees (which was totally untrue as his mother had paid the fees in advance). He assured her that as soon as the funds from his mother arrived, he would return the money to her. He repeated this lie to her several times and the girl gave him a total of £800 on three separate occasions. This confirmed the three visits that the Landlord told me where James would be waiting outside the door for the girl to bring him the money.

I felt the girl was definitely telling me the truth and I assured her that I would do my best to help her get the money back from James. By then, James was already studying in the boarding school. I phoned him and asked him again if he had borrowed some money from the girl at the language school. Once again, he denied it. I then told him I had met this girl and I believed he had taken some £800 from her. I asked him to return the money immediately. Again, he denied it.

I had a sleepless night, wondering what to do next. The next morning I decided to ring James' mother again. I asked her to discuss this matter with James and get back to me as I tended to believe the girl's story, having met her in person. The following day, James' mother replied and was still in total denial of the allegation of her son's wrongdoing. She said James had been given pocket money and it was not necessary for him to borrow any money.

I thought deeply about the matter and felt that James and his mother could not get away with their deceitful behaviour. I called James' mother again and this time I spoke in a much more determined manner. I told her I believed the girl and, if she did not send £800 to my bank account so I could return it to the girl, I would put this matter in the hands of the police and also write to the Home Office if James was convicted. This would mean that James would be sent back to China and his visa cancelled. He would also be put on a blacklist so he would never be allowed into the UK again.

My threat worked! The next day, I received James' mother's reply confirming that the money James owed was on the way to my account. I was absolutely delighted that justice had been done. On receipt of the funds, I went to see the girl and returned the £800 to her. I also advised her to be really careful in future and not to trust anyone so easily with her money.

This story has stuck in my mind for a long time. I wondered how James was going to live this lie for the rest of his life, being two years younger than he truly was. Surely, he would have to be honest with his future wife and family and perhaps his doctor too.

Being a guardian to someone's child, with a strong determination to treat him or her like your own, was never easy. You did not know anything about their family background and how they were brought up. All you knew was that Chinese parents all had ambition for their children to go to one of

England's best schools and universities. They could then become either a doctor or a lawyer. Very few parents would be happy for their children to go into the arts, music or theatre performance. I remember one violin teacher at an excellent school told me that once the child was in the school, parents would like their children to finish learning their instruments up to Grade 8 and no further. They sometimes even openly told the violin teacher that he should not encourage their children to aim for music for a degree, or worse, as a career, even if he or she had a special talent. That would not do, so the violin teacher was warned.

So it was rather unusual for me to relay the story of Fred here. This email from him before leaving his school to go to Oxford University to study History was very heart-warming and made me realise how worthwhile my hard work was.

"Dear Mrs. Clarke,

As you know my results came out a while ago and I was fortunate enough to score D2D2A, with only 2 marks off an A* in Latin. I had prepared a card to give to you as a token of my gratitude, but I was told that since you did not know about the card, you had mistaken my thoughtful preparation as a sign of ungratefulness. Hence, I decided to transfer my message from the card to this email. I deeply appreciate the advice that Mr. Clarke and you have given me regarding university and no doubt your initial lack of confidence in my application along that of Dr. Bessant spurred me on to put more effort in the process than I otherwise would have. I would also like to take this opportunity to thank you for the help you offered as my guardian and for maintaining surveillance over my academic performance over the past five years, as well as taking care of me and arranging various host families prior to the purchase of our Cambridge home. Your efforts are irreplaceable, and I am glad that our student-guardian relationship ended with my 'blossoming' and that in the end I was able to fulfil my promise that everything would be fine in the end. It has been a very intuitive experience studying under your guardianship and I hope other students of yours would appreciate it as much as I did.

Kind regards,

Fred"

I became Fred's guardian when he joined the school at the age of thirteen. He came from Beijing but had spent a couple of years in Singapore prior to coming to UK. This had given him an excellent foundation in English, and so he gained a place at one of England's top boarding schools without much difficulty. His mother Amy, whom I got to know and formed a close friendship with over many years, was a writer of short stories. When she was in China, her writing was published, and she had quite a large following. She was a very sophisticated, soft spoken Chinese lady. She always dressed herself in white, without any jewellery, as to demonstrate her purity and freedom from contamination of materialism.

She told me that she was living in Singapore while Fred was being educated there whilst her husband remained in China. When she met her husband, Shen, before their marriage, he was one of her readers. He wrote to her as he admired her work and that was how they met.

Shen started off as a bank clerk. During the economic revolution in China, Shen had the opportunity to get involved with a group of rich and powerful people who trusted him and used him to front some of their projects, turning former State enterprises into profitable commercial enterprises and floating some of their companies on the Stock Exchange. As these projects were all over China, Shen became a very busy businessman, so Amy took sole responsibility for the care and education of their one and only son. Shen became very successful in his dealings and became rich, owning several properties in Beijing. I have had the opportunity to visit his offices and two of his flats. Everywhere he lived and worked glittered with gold.

As China's economy grew and many men were now in possession of large amounts of wealth, morality suffered. Large amounts of strong alcohol were often consumed at business dinners and women from poorer family backgrounds used these wealthy businessmen as bait to improve their living standards. That period of time marked the start of the increase of luxurious consumer products in China. I understand it was common, or even fashionable, for men who were already married and had a family, to start having girlfriends. Wives were told this was part of their husbands' business activities and they would have to learn that times had changed and understand. Many wives found it difficult to accept but, as they had tasted a much more comfortable lifestyle than they had before, they found this a bitter pill to swallow but they were told it was for their own good.

Amy invited me to tea one day and broke the sad news that her husband was having a relationship with one of his secretaries. Loyal staff to her in the office had disclosed the information to her. She broke down when she heard the news and confronted Shen. As you could expect, he told her that it was quite normal in the society for men to have girlfriends. What's more, as Amy was away a lot caring for Fred, he did not consider there was anything wrong. He had tried to be loyal to Amy until one evening when he was quite drunk, his secretary came into his room to help him and that was the beginning of their affair.

Being an honourable, totally moral and pure wife, Amy found the situation painful to bear but for the sake of Fred, she was prepared to try to resolve the situation. She asked Shen to dismiss the secretary right away. Shen asked Amy to give him time as he was in the midst of a project which took time to complete.

Amy gave him time to sort things out whilst she continued to focus her attention on Fred. In the meantime, friends of Amy who worked in Shen's office continued to feed information to her. They told Amy that this secretary was determined to make herself indispensable and continued to accompany Shen on all his business trips.

Amy even found a website started by a group of mistresses supporting each other's objectives of capturing wealthy boyfriends and eventually stealing them away from their wives and families. How on earth could she, a simple and naïve woman, fight this foul culture to save her own marriage!

In the end, it was clear that Amy's marriage with Shen was over and the more so when she found out that Shen and his secretary were now starting another family. To compensate for his wrongdoing, Shen gave Amy a fairly large settlement. Part of the sum was used by Amy to purchase a property in the UK and soon she was also able to apply for a visa to live permanently in the UK where Fred continued his education.

I continued to support Amy in her distress and sorrow and, although she lived in the UK, she insisted that I should continue to be Fred's Guardian. I agreed as I knew Amy did not fully understand the UK education system and needed guidance. She was also not very confident in her spoken English. What's more, Amy told me that now Fred had turned a teenager, he would no longer listen to her. She said I only had to tell him once and he would take note.

Fred was an extremely intelligent boy. His English was excellent and therefore he had absolutely no problems with all the other subjects. During one half-term school break, when Amy was in China, I placed Fred in a host family. I had a phone call from the host family one evening advising me that Fred was totally addicted to computer games at their home. He would be on the computer in his pyjamas from morning until past mid-night. This had been happening since he arrived, and they felt they had no alternative but to turn off the power in his room! The next day, I had a strong word with Fred. I stressed that after this half-term, he had a mock exam coming and he should use his time well to revise.

I attended Fred's parent-teachers' meeting after the mock exam results were issued. They were all B's which, in normal circumstances for a Chinese student whose English was less strong, I would be pleased, but not for Fred. I was furious when I met him. I asked if he had done any revision as I advised. He was honest and said he hadn't. I told him he was a very intelligent boy with a great future and the possibility of going to one of the top universities in the world, like Cambridge or Oxford. If he did not even make any effort, he would not achieve it and would have totally wasted this golden opportunity.

Amy rang me in the evening and told me that Fred told her that I had spoken to him in a very severe manner and that no one had ever spoken to him like that. Amy was supportive and thought that was good for Fred, as she had tried to encourage him to work hard too, but to no effect.

I think Fred had taken my remarks on board and passed his GCSE reasonably well with at least seven A stars which was the minimum number to have any chance to go to Oxbridge. In the Sixth Form, Fred started to take responsibility for his learning. He had started to mature, and he excelled particularly in history, which he loved. He applied to Oxford and there were nine other students who also applied. Fred was the only one who was successful. I was absolutely thrilled.

Fred's intellectual ability grew with him. He went on to obtain a Master's degree in the History of Art and I heard last year that he had been successful in gaining some funding to do a PhD in the History of Art. Going down the Arts path was not eligible for many Chinese students, but for Fred, with family wealth and a totally supportive mother, he had this option open to him. Very sadly though, Fred refused to speak to his father after the breakdown of his parents' marriage.

Amy now lives in the UK permanently. She took English and French lessons. She also started to paint and has resumed her writing.

More and more foreign students came under my guardianship from schools within ninety miles of Cambridge. Some of these students were introduced via parents while many others came directly from school registrars. As the services required of a guardian, such as parent/teachers' meetings or visits to host families, took place in the evenings or weekends, it worked well with the family's needs. Our boys were growing up and it was possible to leave them at home on their own as I was confident there would not be a problem. At this stage, Peter had accepted a position as a Bursar where he had to reside near the school, which was located in Colchester, some sixty miles away.

I recalled after a parents' evening meeting at a school over sixty miles away from our home, I telephoned home after the meeting had finished. Our younger son, Henry, picked up the phone. I told him I was leaving the school now and would be home in about an hour. On arriving home, Henry had already warmed up the meal which I had prepared before I left, so they could eat before me. He quickly prepared two places on the table. I was surprised at that and asked why he had not eaten. He said he had had some, but he wanted to keep me company. This was one of the sweetest memories of Henry as a young teenager. Some parents warned me when the boys were much younger and were then as good as gold that I should wait until they became a teenager. I wished I could remind them of their warning to me, that it wasn't true.

It was interesting to mention that my reputation as a guardian was always much valued and favoured by the schools and the parents. They knew I was reliable and would always be there when needed. On the other hand, some students were rather fearful when they learned that the school and parents had chosen me to look after them, as they had been told that I was very strict. Parents told me that I was exactly what they wanted as it would be difficult for them to monitor their children's progress thousands of miles away. Moreover, they were not familiar with the UK School education system. Often, they would consult me over choice of subjects or university.

As I took a serious interest in the children's learning and progress, I was always at their schools to attend parents/ teachers' meetings and I enjoyed speaking to their teachers. As I was a third party to the children's education, teachers felt they were often able to speak openly to me and not try to find words to describe the children's progress in a roundabout way to their parents, especially when their children weren't doing at all well. I was, thus, able to know many teachers at the various schools well. Sometimes, they would volunteer to give me news about other children under my guardianship at parents/ teachers' meetings. So, I knew in advance the information about the children's good behaviour, or wrong doings, before the news reached their parents.

I found a good way to keep an eye on my students, who were often too relaxed about their work, was to contact their Tutors and urge them to put pressure on them. Tutors saw their tutees at least once a week, if not twice a week. They could also speak to other teachers in the Common Room to find out information about their tutees. I was quite amused when one of my students told me that his Tutor came into his study one evening and spoke to him quite severely saying: "You must get your act together to work hard, as your guardian is on my back!"

Another interesting case of how well I was able to serve my students related to Nicholas (Nic), a teenager from Indonesia of Chinese descent. He was the only son in the family with three older sisters. As one could imagine, it was easy for him to be spoiled. The family was quite wealthy and Nicholas knew that it wasn't probably that important for him to work hard. He was quite clever and often just did enough to avoid trouble from his teachers. He was very sociable and made many friends at school and settled into boarding school life happily.

One day, I had a telephone call from the Head's secretary, in a rather urgent manner, that the Head wanted to see me as soon as possible, and it was about Nic. It happened that the call came to my mobile phone whilst I was already at school attending a school concert. So, I was able to arrive at the Head's office almost instantaneously which was impressive. The Head told me that a woman, unrelated to his school, had rung him and said that her son, who was not at his school, informed him that his good friend, who was attending the Head's school, was being bullied frequently by a boy called Nicholas (Nic) at school. Her son said that his friend didn't want to report him for fear for reprisal. But this woman thought the situation had to be reported back to the school to protect her son's friend. This woman added that she heard Nic purposely closed the lap top computer hard on the boy's hand. After a thorough investigation by the Housemaster of the boy involved and speaking to Nic, the Head told me he was thinking of expelling him. This would be devasting as Nic had just started the Upper Sixth Form and A-Level exams were a stone's throw away. I asked the Head if he could give me a little time to talk to Nic which he did.

Nic admitted to me that he had been verbally abusing this boy whom he felt was constantly annoying him. Nic then disclosed to me that he had recently heard that his parents were going to get a divorce. His mother was being investigated for the possibility of cancer whilst his father's business was in serious trouble. His father had purchased oil forward at a high rate and the price had now fallen through the roof. So, when this boy at his house said something to annoy him, he lashed out his frustration. He did apologise to him and was fully contrite over what he had done. Whilst Nic had always appeared to be a relaxed, happy-go-lucky type of teenager, he was actually hiding behind a dark tunnel which he was about to go through back at home. He didn't tell anyone about his family difficulties, and this was the first time he spoke about it.

I was very sympathetic with Nic when I heard his side of the story and I relayed that to the Head and asked if he would allow him to stay in school to finish his A Levels which was important to him. I assured him that I would check out Nic's story with his sister whom I communicated with regularly. The Head was in agreement with my suggestion and the next day, following my telephone call with Nic's sister, I confirmed that all the facts were correct. I was very pleased the Head let Nic continue his education there, but he had to take some punishment. He had to work in the School Library whenever he had free time in his timetable for a month. I thought the Head was really wise and gave the good news to Nic's sister, who promised she would speak to Nic about his behaviour.

As the guardianship business was developing well and we were now able to finance the boys' education, which was my highest priority, I decided it was time to leave my conference manager's job and focus even more on the guardianship side. The College salary was very modest, especially working part-time. I recall my elder son questioned me one day why I was still working in the College with the fairly healthy number of students I was serving. I told him that I enjoyed the work and, jokingly, it was convenient to have a free car park in the centre of town!

Before I resigned, I told Charles, the Bursar, that the annual turnover of the conference trade, after working there for nine years, part-time, was a grand total of £360,000. All the bedrooms and meeting rooms were utilised for over ninety per cent of the time during the Easter and summer vacation. This was in contrast to my understanding of what the Bursar told me a few months earlier that the conference business wasn't growing. Anyway, I thought I needed to tell the Bursar the size of our business portfolio before I left the College as I was unsure how much he knew. Four months later, I had a call from the Bursar asking if I would be able to speak to the Police if they needed to question me. Apparently, Robert, the clerk in charge of the bills and some cash generated by the students' bar, was caught stealing College funds! He took a rather big amount, but they weren't sure of the exact amount. It could be up to £40,000. I was shocked but at the same time relieved to hear that, and, jokingly, I asked the Bursar if he would be prepared to adjust the bonus which I was supposed to have, had he received the correct accounting information. We both had a laugh as Charles was aware that my own business was doing well.

Several months after I left the College, I had a call from the Bursar again. This time he said he needed my help urgently. He said the Admissions Secretary was taken seriously ill and the Senior Tutor needed someone he could trust to take over right away. Without hesitation, I agreed. I thought it would be an eye-opener to work in the Admissions Office to see how things were done. After all, it would not be many years before it was our son's turn to choose a university. I immediately agreed but once again, on a part-time basis.

Mark was the Admissions Tutor. He was a mathematician and was very quiet and shy. My role was to arrange all the necessary application papers orderly in separate files, after entering their personal information and academic records into the data file. It was amazing to see first-hand the high numbers of A and A* grades each of these candidates had achieved. It was also interesting to learn that in some small subjects, for example veterinary medicine or architecture, only one in twelve candidates would be successful. In popular subjects such as Law, Medicine, Engineering or Natural Sciences it would be one in five. Classics, Music or Theology were the least competitive, one in three.

At the time when I was working there, over seventy per cent of the candidates applying would be from the private schools, although only seven per cent of the student population in the UK. were in private schools. Today, the situation has reversed which was made possible with the much-improved government schools.

I was keen to find out how the Directors of Studies for the various Degree Courses select their students since almost all of them seemed well suited. Before the interview took place, I had to prepare interview forms where candidates were marked out of ten. Anyone achieving seven or above was immediately on the acceptance list. Six was questionable, and below that was a definite no.

The interview was in two parts. The first part was to have a general conversation with the Admissions Tutor. The second and more important part was to have an academic interview with the subject Director of Studies and another colleague from the Department. This was where students felt they were being grilled. Each interview took no more than twenty minutes.

Most subjects would have a written test as well before the interview, so the success was not purely based on school reports and public exams grades. I felt it was a totally thorough and fair process. I had the chance to speak to one of the two key admissions tutors and asked her how they could choose, as all the candidates I processed had straight As. She told me that she was looking for candidates with potential. They should be like a strong springboard such that they could easily jump over academic hurdles, as all Cambridge Degrees were very demanding. She was also looking for candidates' passion. How independently they were able to work and more importantly, what sort of books they read regularly. She also said that she would make allowances for students coming from UK's top public schools, like Eton, Harrow and the like because these candidates would have been well-prepared and polished for their interviews. In summary, the College tried to be very fair to every candidate and only the strongest academic scholars would be suitable.

I was pleased I was able to work in the Admissions Office for a whole academic year which gave me the opportunity to gain some insight into what Cambridge University was looking for. It was a particularly tense moment when A-Level results came out. Ninety-nine per cent of offer conditions made by the university were met by the selected candidates but there was one I recalled who was unsuccessful. She came from a State Comprehensive School in a poor area of the country and she missed the required grades. Mark, the Admissions Tutor, learned that there were serious family and health issues involved, after speaking to her school. He was extremely sympathetic and agreed to hold the place for her if she were to repeat the subject and improve it to an 'A' grade. It was good to see the humanity side of a somewhat stern Admissions Tutor before I left this interesting post. Sadly,

I had to finally say good-bye to my private beloved car park in the centre of town!

Sidney Sussex College, Cambridge

10

CAMBRIDGE PROGRAMMES

HAVING GAINED such valuable experience on the conference and admissions areas of a Cambridge College, I was interested to see if I could start a summer programme myself. I thought it would be a wonderful opportunity for students in Hong Kong or China to taste what life in a Cambridge College was like and perhaps inspire them to apply.

I had learned a lot about how summer schools were organised during my role as a Conference Manager. This included an American summer school who came to us every year. Taryn, the director, brought hundreds of American teenagers from all over the United States and placed them in different Cambridge Colleges. I was astonished to learn that her summer school had over 800 students. I accommodated 150 of them which was our full capacity and they stayed for three weeks. The revenue of this summer school contributed a large and profitable income for the College.

I found that the director of the summer programme, Taryn, was exceedingly disorganised and I was intrigued to know how she managed to recruit such a large number of students to join her. I learned from her assistant, whom I got to know well, that Taryn had a contact in the American Education Board. He would provide Taryn with the names of those students who required further credits before they were eligible to apply to Colleges.

So that was why she was able to target this vast list of students into her programme. Because Cambridge was such an attractive place to visit, especially in the summer, Taryn attracted all types of high school students too.

Taryn's daughter was married to a Cambridge Fellow, and through his connections she was able to recruit academics to teach various subjects, which was impressive. Her students could choose which lectures they were interested to attend. Students were also assigned a mentor in the ratio of one mentor to ten students. Our son, Charles, was offered a job as a mentor for Taryn. It was interesting to learn from him first-hand how the programme was run, as an insider!

One day, I came across one of Taryn's lecturers who was a PhD student called Richard in our College. He told me that Taryn had only contacted him the night before to give a morning lecture. I didn't think that was very good practice and Richard told me that he was not the only one. A few of his friends too were given almost no notice. They were, however, paid handsomely!

As this was a summer school from abroad and, with my previous banking experience, I felt it would be prudent for me to charge Taryn the full fees in advance, rather than just take a normal deposit. I was delighted that I adopted this strategy as I found out, years later, that some Colleges' bills were left unpaid. Not only was our College account fully paid and we even had a small surplus!

Having learned that even such a poor organisation could be successful, I was determined to give the idea of starting a summer school in Cambridge myself serious consideration. I spoke to Richard and asked if he would be interested to work with me to start a summer programme for Chinese students. I would be responsible for marketing and he would be in charge of the academic side.

Through my contacts with Chinese parents in China from my guardianship services, I was aware of the fast economic growth in China and that private businesses were flourishing. Like me, Chinese parents would always put their children's education as a top priority and would be prepared to invest in their children.

I thought with the one-child policy in China, parents would be keen to have their one and only child involved in the family business in the hope that they would eventually take over when they retired. Hence, I thought it would be rather innovative to start a three-week mini-MBA programme to give children some idea of what qualities they needed in order to be successful in business. I knew this was not something schools offer.

Although Richard's own research was not on the business side, he had several friends in Cambridge's Business School, the Judge Institute of Management. He said he would speak to them to see if they would be interested to help us teach. Within a short period of time, Richard came back to me and said all his friends at the MBA School were happy to be involved.

I was delighted with his initial findings and decided to arrange a marketing trip to China. I consulted my student Charles' father, who had a lot of influence in Shanghai. He said he would be very happy to help me locate some prospective schools. Although he himself did not have direct contacts with school Heads, he had a friend, Jennifer, who had. Very quickly, a programme of school visits was arranged for me.

As my proposed mini-MBA Programme was considered to be rather expensive in the Chinese market at the time, it was thought that I might have a better chance of success to market it to some of the newly opened private secondary schools in China. I was fascinated to meet the Heads of these schools. They all looked more like "businessmen" than the headmasters I was familiar with in the UK. None of them spoke much English. Their school premises and grounds were huge and extensive. I recall seeing one school had a bright, glittering golden apple, nearly five metres high, displayed right at the front of the school entrance, as Golden Apple was the name of the school!

The heads all acknowledged my idea was a good one (since they all owned businesses but probably had never been to a Business School). Then I was introduced to other senior staff members to discuss further details. More meetings took place but I was unable to get a date as to when I could present my programme to the parents. In the end, it was clear to me that the Schools would only promote our programme if they were offered some financial inducement. I was totally opposed to this idea as it would culminate in a form of bribery. I definitely did not want to go down that route.

I also took Richard to visit some of the well-known secondary schools I knew in Hong Kong to see if they would be interested. Sadly, the schools told me that business is not a subject they offered at school and so it would be difficult to assign the organisation of such an overseas trip to any subject teacher. With great disappointment, I decided I would have to drop the summer school idea.

How thrilled I was that one day, I received a telephone call from the Head of one of the Jesuit schools in Hong Kong. His name was Mr So. He told me that he was sorry he missed my recent visit to Hong Kong. Having read the leaflet I left for him, he thought his school would be very interested to send some students to Cambridge if I were able to offer them an English Immersion Programme. Since the return of Hong Kong to China, the standard of English had declined rapidly. He told me that, unlike other schools, his teaching philosophy was to encourage his children to read widely, not just load them with tons of homework or tests. He would also like his students to gain overseas experience to widen their horizons. He had one teacher in his school who would be very happy to lead this trip, if I could organise it. I thought Mr So was a visionary and I was, therefore, keen to support his educational ideas.

I told Mr So that I would give his proposal some serious thought and get back to him. I said I had no interest in running an English language summer programme, like many others in Cambridge. I had learned a huge amount about education, working in a Cambridge College for nine years, visiting many fantastic private schools through the guardianship company I ran, as well as following our sons' marvellous education at their very successful school. The aim I had was to design a programme which would be inspirational and would be an excellent academic learning experience for Hong Kong students. I felt that children could learn whilst having fun in the summer, if I could get good teachers and employ some Cambridge educated mentors as their role models. My summer programme would include some of the activities which Cambridge students experienced during Term Time, like a Formal Hall dinner, Choral Evensong or a Burns' Night Supper. More importantly, they should also have the opportunity to hear from a Cambridge Admissions Tutor what Cambridge University was looking for and how they should prepare themselves if they wanted to apply.

Once I had finished drafting a daily timetable for a two-week summer programme, I arranged to visit Mr So's school so I could give a presentation to the parents. There was a brother Jesuit School linked to Mr So's School and he offered to introduce my programme to their school head too. Nearly a hundred parents came when I presented the Programme to these two Jesuit schools and a total of fifty-two boys enrolled in the first year.

I must mention that what was most unusual about this wonderful Head, Mr So, was that he offered five free places

Formal Dinner in a Cambridge College

and five half-fees places to encourage his students to apply. His selection criteria were that these places did not go to the best academic students but to those who had the ability to do well, but were not fulfilling their potential. In fact, he chose students from very modest and humble backgrounds. I remember one of the boys he sent to our programme had never been on a plane before. This boy was fifteen years old. He had a curious mind, was very talkative and very eccentric, earning a nickname called "ET", standing for Extra Terrestrial, on the Programme. ET was the title of a popular science fiction film at the time.

Gary, the teacher who came with the boys, was a very dedicated man in his late thirties. He was a very devout Christian, had no children of his own and it was clear he was a teacher who wanted to dedicate his life to the students. His wife also came along on the trip. She was an organist and a music teacher. She was also very supportive of Gary and his work. Every day, it was thrilling to see how keen Gary was to see his students' progress and how he impressed he was with the way our Programme was being run.

So, the very first Cambridge Programme began in 2004 with 52 boys and four teachers from the two Jesuit Schools from Hong Kong. Our son Charles, who was in his first year at Churchill College, helped to recruit some of his peers to act as Mentors on our Programme. We were offered a block of student rooms at Corpus Christi College, located near the famous King's College, which was ideal. The rooms were not actually inside the College, but located nearby, next to the pub where Francis Crick, a Nobel Prize winner who developed DNA, met with his colleagues to discuss his research.

Using my extensive contacts at schools, we had no difficulty recruiting some of the best teachers to help devise an English Immersion Programme to suit our Hong Kong students. As they were attending an English-speaking school where English was the medium for teaching all subjects, these students' English ability was generally good, particularly in reading and writing, but less so in their spoken English. The English Programme provided them with an ideal platform to speak English. Our goal was to enable them to experience English academic culture in more depth with an emphasis on Cambridge. The concept was one of hard work leading to academic success for a fulfilling life and to engender the idea of life-long learning in a rapidly changing world.

Our mentors were in charge of organising extra-curricular activities which included a debate in the Cambridge Union, in their famous debating chamber. We also took the students on trips to London and Oxford. There was a lot of fun on the Programme too, such as seeing a musical in the West End and a visit to Shakespeare's Globe theatre in London. Our mentors

End of Programme Presentations

found the first few days very difficult as the students were shy and unwilling to speak. I encouraged the mentors to be patient and continue to show care and compassion. Much to their surprise, within a few days, the students began to come out of their shells and started to form a close bond with their mentors. Mentor groups started to be competitive. I wanted the students to put on a presentation on the final day to give them the opportunity to show off what they had learned. It was a roaring success, and you could hardly recognise that these were the same students who had arrived two weeks before like little mice, completely transformed by their clever mentors! The visiting teachers were very impressed that their students had had such a valuable experience in Cambridge.

I was particularly pleased to learn from ET's teacher, Gary, after the summer, how much ET had changed following his experience on our Programme. His parents were both blue collar workers and would never have dreamt that their son would have the opportunity to go abroad. Gary told me that ET started to work much harder at school and was much more focused in achieving better academic results. He even had an ambition to study in Cambridge one day. Several years later, I was thrilled to learn that ET had been admitted to the University of Hong Kong to read English. He aimed to be a schoolteacher, like Gary. Their son's success had far exceeded his parents' expectations. I told Gary that ET had a lot to thank Mr So, his Headmaster, for his initiative, in addition to his own personal interest in ET's success.

Although everyone on the Programme was happy, I was keen to learn from it and to find ways of further improving it. To start with, I was eager to have some female students to enjoy the experience on our Programme too. If we were successful in increasing our numbers, I would prefer to have our students housed in rooms "inside" the main College, rather than a peripheral place. Unfortunately, when I tried to negotiate the price of the room rental of the College the following year, they wanted to increase the rate by fifty per cent, which was not something we could manage. I was keen not to over-charge the students as this would preclude less well-off parents from sending their children to Cambridge.

First of all, I had to start recruiting girls. I recall when I was working at Girton College, I met a retired ex-Head of a reputable girls' school in Hong Kong. Her name was Kay. The school had an excellent reputation under her headship. She was a missionary who went to Hong Kong some fifty years ago to teach Maths in one of the best co-educational schools in Hong Kong. It was important to note that she herself was one of the first group of Cambridge women allowed to get a Cambridge Degree in 1948! After teaching for a few years, the Bishop back in the UK asked her to head this girl's school. As I expected, she was keen for her girls to come to Cambridge during the summer. This was the beginning of girls arriving from Hong Kong to attend Cambridge Programmes. Every year, the Head, now retired and living in Cambridge, would come to attend our Formal Hall dinner and she would hold a meeting with her girls. The girls would interview their ex-Head and their report would be published in their school magazine.

A few years later, I heard that an alumna of this girls' school had offered Kay's school a handsome donation to thank her specially for believing in her. This sum was used to fund some of the girls to join our Programme. When this alumna was a student at her school, she was not focusing on schoolwork and was frequently in trouble with her teachers for not handing in homework, and talking too much in class. Several teachers went to see the Head to ask for her to be expelled. The Head spoke to the girl and following this, she began to change her behaviour and took her work much more seriously. She stayed out of trouble with her teachers until she left the school. She told the Head she was interested to work in the media and someone from the school gave her an introduction to a radio station. With her talent, she became a very famous radio DJ and was exceedingly successful for many, many years. Everyone in Hong Kong would listen to her popular radio show called: "I am Yu — your Pal!"

The same year, the Head also introduced me to another Head of a girls' school she knew well. With her introduction, two girls' schools joined us the following year. Our number nearly doubled in that year. I decided to approach Sidney Sussex where I used to work and asked if they could accommodate us. The transition to another College was very smooth. There were enough rooms in College to separate girls from boys' accommodation.

With girls on the Programme, I felt the boys, coming from a single sex school, would have benefitted more in class and particularly in debating, for example. Girls were, in general, more serious in their learning than the boys. The Programme, into our second year, was again a success. All the students, and their teachers, were happy.

In my review at the end of this Programme, there were only a couple of minor issues which concerned me. As the College was opposite a large supermarket, the students were able to pop across the road to buy huge amounts of unhealthy snacks and Coca-Cola frequently. Putting on the hats of their parents, I felt this was not such a good idea and it was impossible for me to stop this. As the College was right in the city centre, it was also far too open to the public. On one occasion, a stranger managed to follow one of our students into her staircase. Although she came to no harm, I was terrified, and I thought it would be safer to move our Programme to a College further away from the centre of town.

The reputation of Cambridge Programmes continued to grow and, with our yearly marketing trips to Hong Kong, the numbers continue to increase. On the third year, we had around 150 students. We managed to move to another College outside the city centre, exclusively for our use during our two weeks in the summer vacation.

Although the students on our Programme were really enjoying the lessons and the activities, I was beginning to face new challenges from the accompanying teachers from their schools. They were asked by their schools to accompany their students and because this was part of their summer holidays, some of the less responsible teachers treated the trip very much as their own summer break. This was fine with us as we were very happy with the Mentors looking after the students so carefully. Students began to form a close bond with their Mentors after a few days and did not particularly wish to see their teachers. Unfortunately, some of their teachers were not on time for coach trips, or went off for a day's shopping. Occasionally when students were unwell, we were not able to advise them straight away. It was very important to communicate such information very rapidly because the student's worried parents would be on the line wanting to know all the details.

Some teachers were unfamiliar with the English protocol and started taking photographs of our mentors and other students without prior approval! This was very tricky to handle. I did not feel comfortable criticising the teachers too severely as they would probably be asked to report back to the Head how our Programme went.

I recall one year, on the last day, one of the schoolteachers disappeared before the coach had to leave for the airport. We searched for this teacher everywhere, but he was nowhere to be found. I thought we had no choice but had to leave this teacher behind. Unfortunately, he had all his students' passports with him. Everyone was beginning to panic and then I saw the teacher walking up the road in a relaxed manner. Apparently, he had not read his timetable about the coach's departure! Phew...

I was in a dilemma about what I should do the following year to change the teachers' behaviour without repercussions on the student intake. I consulted Kay and asked her advice. She was most sympathetic about the situation, and she advised me to write down exactly what I expected of the teachers. It seemed straightforward but not necessarily so.

On my yearly school visits, it was clear some teachers were keen to come but some with young families were not. As years passed, some schools, which were regular participants, ran out of teachers to send to our Programme, which was totally understandable. I had, therefore, to be flexible and started giving permission for some married members of staff to bring their wives or husbands if they wished to accompany them. This flexibility did help to solve the problem for the school. Whilst the teachers and their partners paid for their own airfares, all their accommodation and tickets for outings etc. were absorbed as part of our Programme costs. I understand some schools even gave their teachers £400 as pocket money. Even with written instructions and individual timetables distributed to teachers, it was disappointing that sometimes, one or two of them were late for coach departures on our excursions. But at least, everyone was there when the coach departed for the airport with their students' passports. It was a relief!

Whatever the difficulties we had from the visiting adults, I was determined that the programme must continue, and the quality continued to improve year after year. I felt it was extremely valuable in different ways to the students and therefore not to worry too much about the teachers who gave us their time in the summer holidays.

It was worth mentioning that during the Programme, we included a fund-raising event to support a charity which involved setting up schools in Ethiopia, one of the poorest countries in the world. It was heart-warming to know that one year, one of the visiting teachers donated his allowance of £400 to the charity! The amount of donations we managed to raise, because of our hardworking and supportive Mentors, exceeded a thousand pounds, which was very pleasing, as the money would allow hundreds of students in Ethiopia to attend schools and have a modest lunch there. The charity I supported was run by a Catholic mission. I understand that some of the children walked for two hours to reach their school. The school was so poor that they could only afford to feed the younger children and it was done in an enclosed area. Older children had to do without any lunches, or they had brought their own piece of bread.

The number of students kept increasing year after year such that, the following year, we had to accommodate the students in two different Colleges, which were fairly close to each other. The boys were in one and the girls in another. It was another resounding success. The new College we stayed in was extremely impressed by how well our Programme was conducted. Students were very well behaved, and our Mentors were very capable and reliable. They told me how different we were from other summer schools in the College. I think the main reason was that, after being a Conference Manager for nine years, I was now sitting on the opposite side of the desk. I knew exactly what the College needed and provided everything for them on time and very efficiently. They just followed our instructions and the whole programme ran very smoothly.

I was always pleased when the porters told me, year after year, at the end of our Programme, how fast the time had passed and once again complimented us on the behaviour of our children, how polite they all were and how good their English was. I remember on one occasion, one of the porters mended a pair of spectacles that our student dropped. The Porter taped up the shattered lens for her so that she could see for the rest of the

Programme. The Mentors, too, were highly complimented. They were always hands-on to help when and wherever it was needed. For example, they would move the heavy tables in the Hall for the staff after Burns' Night supper, so our students could use the Hall for Scottish dancing. It was so thrilling to see how much our students looked up to their mentors as role models and treated them like an older brother or sister. From what I was witnessing during the two weeks, I could see that the students were already changing, their aims for their future were lifted. There was a big bubble in their heads and a big dream appeared which was not there before they arrived. This was evident when the Programme ended in that almost every student had tears in their eyes and waved good-bye vigorously from their coach windows. I always went up to the coach to say good-bye to the children and felt a lump in my throat too!

As we had now moved into a college with an excellent reputation for Science, Peter's own College where he read Engineering, he suggested we should offer a Science Programme next year. Once again, we searched through our contacts at various excellent schools and designed an interesting and fun scientific programme. We included a visit to the Science Museum in London, to the Institute of Astronomy in Cambridge and to climb 305 steps up a wind turbine in Swaffham, which has now sadly closed. A Cambridge science lecturer joined us every year to offer the children a murder mystery where the students needed to think hard, based on the evidence they were given, as to who was the murderer. The result of their success was the reward of an enormous fake diamond!

As the colleges do not have laboratories, we searched for nearby schools which would be able to rent us their labs and their lab technician for two weeks. We were fortunate that not only were we successful, but we were able to use some of the enthusiastic science teachers they had. One of these teachers, James, conducted a Chemistry experiment which involved a great explosion which he did outside the lab. Another teacher did an experiment on human digestion which was gruesome to watch but certainly the students learned something they would never forget!

Up to this point, we were only accepting students from secondary schools, aged thirteen and above. It was a surprise when I received a call from Clare, one of the teachers in a Hong Kong School which had joined us two years earlier. She advised me that she had left her school and had since been working in a very exciting Primary School which had an excellent reputation.

The Head of her school was ambitious and very non-traditional. Clare asked if she could bring her Year 6 students, aged eleven, to join our Programme. I had, indeed, heard of this famous Head who had a radio programme giving tips to parents about the education of their young children. My immediate thought was that her students were probably too young, unless they had excellent English. Also, I would need to check if the college was happy to accept residents of this age. Clare gave me her guarantee that her students had excellent English and would enjoy the experience in Cambridge.

After consulting with the conference manager of the college we intended to use to accommodate the junior programme, I was pleased to learn that she would be happy to accommodate them, after she had checked up on us with another conference manager. She heard that our students were very well supervised and our Mentors were totally reliable. It was worth noting that college rules stipulated that they would not normally accommodate residents under the age of sixteen and so we were very privileged indeed to be welcomed.

I gave Clare the good news, but I told her that I would like to have other Primary Schools to come along too, so her students would not be learning on their own. Clare approached her Head and, on the following marketing trip, I was able to give presentations to several equally reputable Primary Schools. So, with the endorsement from the college on the accommodation side and my belief in Clare, the Cambridge Junior Programme was born.

As the students on the Junior Programme were much younger, it was important to design a Programme to suit their needs. I thought the Programme should incorporate English, Science, History and Art. This would prepare them well when they stepped into their secondary schools after the summer holidays. It was also important to encourage intellectual curiosity, to think and learn independently. This, I believe, would serve them well throughout life. This was the quality I myself lacked when I was studying in Hong Kong. We were all learning by rote and never questioned our teachers. When I had to make comments on an English or History essay, I had absolutely no idea how to think.

I thought the Junior Programme should be fun too. A Harry Potter-style formal dinner was introduced before the Programme ended. I thought the Mentors would be brilliant in organising this and they were. The college manager was also very supportive and helped to create an authentic atmosphere in their dining hall. First of all, I needed to find some authentic gowns and, after some investigation, I managed to locate a factory in China to make them. The gowns were delivered directly to the schools in Hong Kong so the children could bring them over. We also took the children to the Harry Potter Theme Park which was an intensely exciting trip for them.

I recall I had a chance to speak to an Admissions Tutor when I was a conference manager. He told me that he was encouraging much younger children to visit the University which surprised

Let's reach for the moon!

me. He said it was important to plant seeds early! So, I was totally convinced that it was right to open our Programme to younger students, to plant a seed in their heads about aiming for Cambridge University, one of the best Universities in the world, after they finished their secondary schools. If they had this in their young minds, even if they did not succeed, they would still be able to attend another very good university.

The students on our Junior Programme all had good English, to the surprise of the college staff where they stayed. They all complimented us on how polite our young students were. We rented some classrooms and a laboratory at a school nearby and they travelled each morning by our coaches to their lessons. Like the older students on the Senior Programme, during the first few days in the classrooms, the children were shy and not responsive when the teachers asked them questions. With the brilliant skills and patience of the teaching staff drawing them out, the ice soon melted. Our teachers were very impressed with the speed at which these children were progressing in just two weeks. They were just transformed.

I remember asking Rachel, one of the children, which was her best subject on the Programme. She said History, and she really loved how the teacher taught the subject in class. It was so wonderful to hear, as I felt that it was an important subject, often overlooked by parents in Hong Kong. I recalled that Mr So, the Head who asked me to offer the first English Immersion Programme to his school, told me that no one chose to study History and it was no longer a subject they offered. He said an alumnus had offered him a History prize a few years before and it was never given out. This alumnus was a doctor and, like me, felt History was a very important subject to learn from. It was very sad indeed to hear this from Mr So.

This was what Rachel said after the Programme:

"I still remembered the first day when we had lessons. I wasn't looking forward to learning history at all. I knew that out of all the lessons we are going to have, this is the worst. Little did I know that right after my first lesson, it immediately became my favourite. I never noticed that the Second World War could be so interesting!"

The Junior Programme ran into trouble once again with schoolteachers' reluctance to accompany the children on the trip, even though most of them treated it totally as a summer holiday. This shocking news was told to me after the presentation was organised at the school and I had to find a solution immediately. I felt it was impossible to offer the Programme to parents without teachers accompanying their young children.

It really made me sad to know that the year before, when I had planned a series of lectures for the accompanying schoolteachers, which I thought would be valuable to them, and would be free to the schools, only eight out of thirty teachers attended. This was the more disappointing, since the lectures covered topics such as mental health and safeguarding, an important constituent in Continuous Professional Development. The others hired a coach and were out all day so they could shop at the Bicester Village, a popular shopping centre, near Oxford for brand-named goods. I suspected that having been on our outings and done their shopping, the teachers didn't find the trips for the children exciting for them anymore.

Fortunately, one of the parents, Ben and Connie, in the school's Parent-Teacher Association came to our rescue. Their daughter, Rachel, had come to our Programme in the previous year and now it was their son's turn. Ben was not going to let the teachers deprive his son of a chance to experience Cambridge Programmes. So, he and his wife offered to help and accompany all the children.

It was wonderful to know how supportive the parents were and, even without their schoolteachers, parents were more than happy to let their children come to our Programme under the supervision of other parents.

Ben said in his email to me: "Your Cambridge Programme is irreplaceable with a trip at any other country. It is just of a different level of value creation to the students. Connie and I are truly grateful to have had the chance to learn about your Programme and to have sent Rachel there last summer."

With Ben and Connie's support, that year's Junior Programme was another huge success, and I could not have been happier when I received a copy of the letter from a boy, aged eleven, given to his Mentor on the last day of the Programme.
Woody's (age eleven) letter to his mentor:
"Hi, Today is the last day of my Cambridge Programme trip. I will really miss you, so please don't leave our WhatsApp

group and stay in contact. The truth is that I have ADHD, that is why I have been eating medicine every day, but after a few days, I learnt how to control myself, if I relax myself too much, I will go crazy, and I've also learnt that every action has a consequence behind.

I've really learnt how to behave and how to control myself, but the person who taught me was you! You taught me everything I need and even when you can't understand me, you still try to solve my problem.

You are a great mentor, and I will never forget you. And also, I haven't told you one thing before, you are very beautiful.

Student Woody"

As the success of our Programmes began to spread around schools in Hong Kong, I was surprised to receive an email from a school head in Brisbane, Australia wishing to send her students to us. Apparently, her school was involved in a science conference with Hong Kong schools and she thought it would be a wonderful experience if her students could also participate. This was the start of Australian schools joining Cambridge Programmes. Through this school, we were successful in marketing our Programme to another school in Brisbane. Like some Hong Kong schools, some Australian students were offered scholarships to help finance their trip.

I was absolutely delighted to know that not only was Cambridge Programmes successful in building a bridge for me to visit Hong Kong annually, but another bridge was built to link me from Hong Kong to Sydney, where my parents and siblings lived. It was something I had never dreamed of, to see my family annually, since my home in Cambridge was thousands of miles away from them.

It was not easy to market our programme to schools in Sydney, as none of them had any direct link with schools in Brisbane.

I was, however, determined to keep knocking on school doors, having researched the names of excellent schools, using contacts via family members and friends who had children studying at their schools. Eventually, after three years, my nephews' old school, which was an excellent private school, decided to give us a try. This was the start of a long relationship with this school which promoted our Programmes internally year after year to their parents.

Having Australian students on our Programme, who were very friendly to the Hong Kong students, I could see we had reached a new dimension. The Hong Kong students really liked their Australian counterparts. It was pleasing to see and hear the Hong Kong students chatting freely with Australian students outside classrooms. The teaching staff also reported that the addition of Australian students had improved the atmosphere in class. It was even more pleasing, at the end of Programme concert, to hear Australian students singing "Waltzing Matilda" and Hong Kong students playing their Chinese instruments.

I realised it would be beneficial, for the sake of the Hong Kong students and our teachers, if we were able to recruit students from schools in other countries to taste Cambridge Programmes too. When I was a Guardian, I got to know a brilliant schoolteacher very well, who had gone to head a school in Malaysia. Using his contacts, I managed to get into a Malaysian school, whose head was himself a Cambridge graduate. He had no hesitation in recommending our Programmes to the parents. He wanted very much to beat the Cambridge drum, and, with his support, Malaysian students also came the following year.

The parents whose children were under my guardianship continued to stay in touch and were aware of the birth of Cambridge Programmes. So, they sent their children to join, and advertised our Programmes to their friends in other countries.

Our programmes now had overseas Chinese students from America.

Parents from China now advised me that it was no longer an issue to get visas to travel abroad. This gave me confidence to start approaching schools in China, but I knew it would not be easy. Personal contacts in China were the only way in, for business. What's more, I was still determined that all dealings with Chinese schools would be on the same premise as our other schools in Hong Kong and Malaysia. I was not prepared to offer any financial incentive to the schools. I thought the best route would be to try the international schools which were now quite widespread in China, particularly in large cities, like Shanghai.

One year, we had three Chinese girls join our programme. These girls were already at a boarding school in the UK and I was the guardian for two of them. They had all enjoyed the programmes very much and were inspired. One of the girls was previously in an international school in Shanghai which was ranked one of the best there. When I asked her to introduce me to her old school, she immediately agreed. On her return home for the holidays, she went back to her school and met with the head personally. She told him all about her experience on our fantastic programme and persuaded the head to meet me when I visited Shanghai.

The head was a very charming Englishman who had previously taught in the UK. He himself was a Cambridge graduate and so it was not difficult to convince him of the value of our programmes. However, there was a lot of politics inside the school and the head said he would give permission for us to market our programme to their parents, but it could not be done under the auspices of the school. His idea worked and some of their students joined our Programme.

Through the help of another Chinese parent, we were

successful getting into another large Chinese school which had a large campus and six other school branches. Although we were quietly thrilled to be able to get into another Chinese school, we were careful to ensure that the students all had adequate English language skills in order to gain the benefits of the programme. So we had to test their English and we took only eight out of over twenty keen applicants whose English was not up to our standard.

Having gone more "international" in our recruitment, I felt we needed to offer vocational programmes too, like Law and Medicine for students aged fifteen. This was something parents in Hong Kong had always asked about.

I thought I would like to approach one of our mentors, who was reading Law, whom I had known personally for several years, to be our initial Director of Studies for a law induction programme. She was the daughter of one of my host families. She knew I had experience working in the admissions office in Cambridge and had previously sought my advice when she was in the sixth form. I had suggested that she attended a law conference organised specially for sixth formers by the Law Faculty in Cambridge in the Easter break. It was only a small three-day conference and if she registered early, she might be able to get a place on it. I thought that would help her know more about the Law Course before she applied. She followed my advice and decided to choose law and subsequently applied and got in.

As students had not come across Law in their school curriculum, it would not be too difficult to structure a law induction programme from scratch. Our aim was to give students a more informed understanding of what the study of law at a top university involves. It also helped students to succeed in their university applications and studies, through developing the initial skills required for studying law.

The Law Induction Programme offered an overview of the legal system in England and Wales, and an introduction to aspects of Constitution Law, Criminal Law, International Law, Jurisprudence and Private Law. Cambridge University-style teaching and supervisions were complemented by visits to courts of local and national significance, and there were also opportunities to develop practical skills through mooting (mock-trials) and debating. Students were also given guidance on applying to study Law at university, and on careers after a Law degree. The Law Programme was successful and attracted students from Australia, Hong Kong and Malaysia. Two years ago, when this Law Mentor left the Programme due to her work pressure, I found an even better qualified Director of Studies for Law. He was previously one of our mentors too but was now a law academic.

I was so thrilled to hear this story from a parent whose daughter attended our Law Programme one year. Like many Chinese parents, Law was a very attractive profession for their children. She was, therefore, keen for her daughter to aim to read Law at University. There was a law induction programme in the University of Hong Kong in the summer and she enrolled her daughter there for several weeks. At the end of that programme, her daughter's interest in law had been totally destroyed. It had actually turned her daughter off the subject completely. When she heard about our Law Programme at her daughter's school, she was very keen to beg her daughter to give it another try. As Chinese children were generally rather obedient to their parents, her daughter came to our Law Programme. I was really delighted to hear that we had re-ignited her interest in Law. This mother told me she was most grateful for this second chance for her daughter! (in accordance with her parents' wishes!).

The Medicine Programme was like a dream come true, not just for me, but for numerous parents who enquired, year after year, if we could do one. My immediate response was that, where could you find someone with a strong medical teaching background to run it. It was not something you could take on lightly. There was the theoretical side as well as the practical side of the subject to be taught in order to offer a Programme which would be helpful and meaningful to the students.

Every year, at the end of our Programme, I would always invite an inspirational academic from the University to address our departing students at the Formal Hall dinner on the final evening. It was always an exciting and emotional time for everyone. I felt the talk from our guest speaker would end the whole experience for the students really well, giving them an important message to take home. We hoped that the potential we had unlocked in each and every one of them, would bear fruit. By this time, students' aspirations were already raised to a much higher level, compared with before, having had a splendid Cambridge student as their Mentors for the two weeks, and all the brilliant teaching and knowledge our wonderful teaching staff had imparted to them.

I was particularly impressed by the Master of one Cambridge College. Her sons and ours went to the same school and we got to know each other's family. She was a law professor and had a laser-sharp brain. After a brief conversation with me over dinner about our Programmes, she was able to target her talk at just the right level for our students, which was truly amazing. I still remember one important message she gave our students was to be curious. She mentioned a children's book she read when she was young — *Curiosity Kills the Cat*! This was a simple message but so valuable if put to practice.

Unfortunately, she was unable to come to join our Formal

Hall dinner that particular year, but promised she would find a colleague who would be equally marvellous in addressing our students. She did indeed send us the inspirational speaker we were hoping for.

He held various senior academic posts in the College, including being a Director of Studies for Medicine as well as an admissions interviewer. He was a medical consultant and an expert transplant surgeon specialising in the pancreas. In addition, he was leading a research team of post-doc students in the University hospital, one of the best in the world.

After a brief chat over dinner, he stood up to address our students. From a bag which he had concealed under his seat he took out a human skull which he held up for all to see. This was surely unique for an after-dinner speaker! He asked the students what was the first thing that came into their heads. There was absolute silence in the Dining Hall (where we had nearly four hundred students and parents attending) and you could hear a pin drop! Students who were attending the English Literature Programme shouted out "Hamlet", the Science students who just had solved a murder mystery the night before, shouted "murder" and the Law students were wondering if there was a legal case to be tried!

It was a memorable evening and even more so when, a few days later, this brilliant medical academic called me to say that if I was interested, he would be able to help me run a Medicine Programme. I felt I had won the lottery that day and that was the birth of our Medicine Programme.

With his help, we designed a world-class medical programme to give participants a deep insight into studying medicine and to prepare them for applying to a top medical school. The aim was to give students a unique and realistic experience of what it is like to study medicine and to be a doctor.

In addition to practical and interactive sessions on the main medical sciences and specialties, the course also covered other key topics and areas that are relevant to medicine and healthcare. These included emerging technologies and future developments, ethical and legal issues, team working and communication, presentation and interview skills. The students on the Medicine Programme were closely mentored in small groups by University of Cambridge Medical students who provided support and additional supervision during the sessions and afterwards. I was delighted to hear from this special team of Mentors on our Medicine Programme that they, too, had learned something from our sessions!

Like a flash, it was hard to believe that Cambridge Programmes celebrated its fifteenth anniversary in 2019. We had grown from fifty-two students in the first year to 240 students that year. Over these years, we were thrilled to have had students from Hong Kong, Australia, Malaysia, United States, Switzerland and China.

When I was giving presentations to schools, I always stated the aims and objectives of our programme which was different from others. I felt it was important to stress that "education is the kindling of a flame", a quotation from Socrates. I wanted our participants to be inspired to excel. We focussed on teaching our participants how to think, how to learn, to be curious, ask questions, work hard and play hard. This was possible with our excellent methodology from our brilliant teachers who would stimulate the minds of the children, so they would start to think critically and creatively. Over time, their self-confidence improved. By the various experiments and activities, we would always try to reinforce in them a sense of aspiration and we also stressed the importance of teamwork. Students were always divided into small groups, and they were mixed with students from other schools and other countries. It was wonderful, but sad, to see the bonds they had formed together when the coaches departed from College on the last day. There were always lots of tears, almost too much for anyone to bear.

Every year, I always did a reflection at the end of the Programme when I would spend ten days relaxing on a Greek island. My reflection would include students' and mentors' feedback, what had worked well and what improvements we could make for the following year.

As the number of students was growing year after year, it was vital that we put in place a strong administrative team, in addition to finding the best teaching staff in and around Cambridge to help us. With the strong recommendation of one of my host families (herself a schoolteacher), we invited the deputy head of her school, who had just retired, to join us as our Programme Dean. She had a lot of experience dealing with students as well as teachers. With the Dean living in College, looking after both the Mentors and students, I was now able to get a good night's sleep! She was brilliant and gained the respect of the Mentors very quickly. To support her, we also appointed several Senior Mentors and appointed one of the very experienced Senior Mentors as the Deputy Dean.

A very good organisation was now in place. On the academic side, we had an excellent Director of Studies for each of our programmes. On the operations side, we had a Dean, a Deputy Dean, Senior Mentors and Mentors. We also hired a school matron to look after the students' well-being. This was now a 'Rolls-Royce' programme.

The most important task each year before the Programme started was to find the necessary Mentors. These young Cambridge students were very important to our students — they would be their role models for two weeks. The most important quality I felt they needed was the ability to communicate with the students. They must be practical young people, willing to roll up their sleeves to help at all times. They needed to be understanding and sympathetic as well as being organised. I remember on one occasion, when I spoke to our elder son Charles, about how we conduct our interviews with potential mentors, he remarked that it sounded more difficult than a Cambridge University interview. My reply was that, as College students, when they were tired or fed up, they could put their books down and do something else. With a group of young students looking up at them, they had to be on duty almost 24/7!

Before the pandemic hit the world, I was extremely pleased to be invited by the education arm of the Hong Kong Telephone Company (HKT) to an education conference they were holding in Hong Kong. They were keen to promote a STEM Programme and, after looking at different summer programmes around the world, they wanted to form a business partnership with us.

Apparently, HKT's technological arm provided support to many of the Hong Kong schools, training their teachers how to use I.T. HKT also had millions of customers using their internet and telephone lines. They, therefore, had a huge database of clients. Another exciting opportunity was open to us. We no longer needed the support of only Hong Kong schools but could potentially reach out to the public. The conference took place in the Hong Kong Convention Centre, and we brought our Dean and our Deputy Dean out to join our marketing team. Sadly, with the arrival of Covid-19, we were not able to proceed with this partnership. Looking back, how fortunate we were to be able to celebrate our fifteenth Anniversary of Cambridge Programmes in August 2019!

2019 Cambridge Programmes

2019 Cambridge Junior Programme

11

REFLECTIONS AND LOOKING AHEAD

LIFE IS SO unpredictable. Who could have predicted the onslaught of a world pandemic three years ago? Who knows when this Covid-19 virus will end? It is an excellent reminder to all of us how valuable life is and how important it is to make the best of it.

My late father's criticism of me, which he conveyed to my mother when I was young, that I was an "over-ambitious" child, has stuck in my mind all my life and has been my driving force. I don't think any child can be over-ambitious, and having no ambition leads you nowhere. I believe if you reach for the stars, you could at least reach the moon. We can't control everything in life, but effort is in our own hands.

I believe ambition can be influenced at a very young age. Although my parents were deprived of a good education, I knew from a young age, however, that they had high expectations of their children. As both parents came from large families, they were aware of how the children of their relatives were developing. If our cousins were doing well at school or in their careers, they would tell us about it and thus implied that we should follow their good example. This applied to filial piety—honour and respect to your parents and elders. My mother looked after my grandmother throughout her life. Grandmother passed away in her eighties under her care.

After I moved to the UK, I would occasionally send my mother a present which I had purchased on my holidays abroad (often a blouse or a scarf). I remember one day, one of my sons, who was very young then, asked me why I was sending grandma a blouse? How did I know if she would like the colour or pattern? More importantly, did I expect him to do the same when he grew up? If so, would he know what I would like. I told him that he would know by the time he grew up and he shouldn't worry about it. This was the culture that was deeply ingrained in our family.

The oak tree wall decoration hanging above the fireplace at our home made me reflect on my life every time I looked at it. That seed from which the tree grew was significant. That seed had to be carefully planted, not too close to another tree or plant, which might have a negative impact as the tree grew and required more light, for example. This was why my mother would queue up for hours when I was young such that she could register me in a reputable school, the seed of learning. Hopefully, I would be studying alongside other students whose parents also had similar ambitions for their children.

I often used this analogy when I spoke to parents whose children came under my guardianship. It was not enough just to plant the seed of ambition in their children, like sending them to a good school in the UK. It would be equally important to water the plant, remove the weeds surrounding it and ensure there was sufficient sunlight for it to grow.

When I was in the kindergarten, age four, the music teacher instructed me to tell my mother when I got home that I was "musical". Although I did not understand what she meant, that seed was already planted in my mind. I was inspired by listening to my neighbour playing the piano as I grew older. I was desperate to learn to play the piano, despite the difficult circumstances of a large family, lack of space in the flat and lack of finance. I managed to pay the fees of my piano lessons by tutoring English to a student three years younger than me, so I did not need to burden my father. Determination to succeed was often the key.

Working, starting a family and bringing the boys up have kept me away from my love of the piano for nearly thirty years, but the flame was still there, and it is now possible for me to reignite it where I had left off.

Life has offered me many paths, like the branches of the oak tree. My musical journey was one of these branches. It did require enormous determination and hard work and was a lifetime's work. A few years ago, I was very much inspired by reading Alan Rushbridger's book *Play it Again*. He spoke about the difficulties of playing Chopin's *Ballade* No. 1, as an amateur pianist. He had only six years' experience playing the piano and yet he succeeded to play it whilst attending a music summer school in France.

To celebrate my seventieth birthday, I set myself a goal to play this piece in a concert after lunch at home. I approached my piano teacher about the idea of learning this immensely difficult piece which, in my mind, was an impossible dream. He was himself a fantastic pianist and, as a teacher, he was so, so encouraging. I started learning from the beginning of the piece; then we skipped to the back of the piece and learned it backwards. One day, when I turned the page over, I realised that I had learned the whole piece. It was almost like the Euro tunnel joining up in the middle. I was elated! I ran upstairs to tell my husband, who was in the bath, that I had finished learning the whole piece. The next step was, of course, just as difficult, as I had to learn to play it effortlessly which would be a lifetime's work. I did manage to play it on my birthday but the anxiety of playing that piece dominated my mind the whole day. I was not sure I remembered what I ate at my birthday lunch! But the fact that I had learned to play this beautiful piece stuck in my mind. I did, after the concert was over, feel quite proud of my achievement and I think my family was too. There are many other pieces I would like to learn and now I am much more confident that I could do it and so my music journey continues.

Another branch of the oak tree is my guardianship journey. My early life in the UK was a rather lonely one, without any family support. Whenever the boys used the words "going home" when they were little, I would only think about Hong Kong as being my home. It was at least ten years after living here that I felt Cambridge was and is my home. The feeling that Cambridge was my home was only confirmed when I visited Hong Kong after my parents had migrated to Australia.

Running the guardianship was like building a larger family. I began creating relationships with students and their parents (many of them are life-long friends). Looking back, these students, like my own children, have borne fruit and turned into the golden leaves on my decorative Oaktree, now glittering above my fireplace. I felt very proud every time I looked at them.

Another strong branch of the tree represented the summer programmes I started. All the many, many students from around the world have been enhanced by attending the programmes we offered them. They, having been inspired by their mentors, have prospered and developed golden leaves which would continue to shine for the rest of their lives. I was sure that they would journey on and continue to develop more branches and more beautiful leaves.

In addition to the students on the summer programmes, I got to know so many amazing young Cambridge students, some of whom I am still I touch with, and these are the branches supporting the students on the Oaktree too. As well as the mentors, the Programmes were warmly supported by the many, many brilliant teachers who were the branches too supporting the mentors and their students. These teachers came to help us year after year during their summer holidays. The Summer Programme grew to become a tradition in their lives.

It was truly fascinating to see how these branches grew and intertwined. Life was naturally, at times, challenging; so it was vital to keep up the effort. If the front door appeared closed, try the back door, and don't walk away!

It would be arrogant of me to consider my life a successful one; but I do have a sense of fulfilment every time I look at my oak tree and its glittering golden leaves. There is a sense of hope, which is all that matters!

About the Author

Rebecca Clarke, 洪嘉儀

Rebecca Clarke was born on 23rd May 1949 into a very large Hong Kong family with nine children - four boys and five girls - when Hong Kong was under British colonial rule. Her parents came from China's Fujian Province, and settled in Hong Kong when Japan invaded China.

Being a daughter with Fujianese parents (who believed girls are less important than boys) Rebecca grew up with a strong will to fight for equality, and a determined mind that where there is a will, there must be a way! For example, she started coaching an eleven-year-old boy in English when she was only fourteen, so that she could pay for her own piano lessons without stretching her father's already tight finances.

Rebecca's father was unable to finance her desire to study music in the UK, and he suggested that she took a teacher training qualification instead. Although her application for teacher training college was approved, she decided not to pursue the course, but to follow her own path in life instead.

After attending a secretarial training course, where she achieved speeds of 150 words-per- minute in shorthand, and 100 words-per-minute on a manual typewriter, Rebecca worked her way up in the commercial world before an opportunity arose where she joined an American bank, before moving on to become a Vice President of an Asian bank.

Following her marriage to an English husband, Rebecca moved to Cambridge and brought up two boys, who are both very successful in adult life. One is an investment banker in California, and the other works for a large pharmaceutical company in Switzerland.

Whilst living in Cambridge, Rebecca established two educational businesses: Cambridge Guardians (where she looked after hundreds of overseas students attending boarding schools) and an inspirational, academically-focused Summer Programme offering English, History, Law, Medicine and Science to students from all over the world. Cambridge Guardians was sold to a new owner in 2017, and Cambridge Programmes celebrated its fifteenth Anniversary in 2019.

Today, over 300,000 Hong Kong residents who have British National Overseas status are allowed to come to the UK, and can become permanent residents after a few years. It is important to know that there are opportunities in the UK for Hong Kong people who have skills to offer the country, who have an entrepreneurial spirit, and who are determined to work hard. You don't have to own a Chinese takeaway, as many did in the past!

CPSIA information can be obtained
at www.ICGtesting.com
Printed in the USA
BVHW062205170223
658734BV00023B/1411/J